Portrait of a Decade

1900-09

ELIZABETH CAMPLING

B.T. Batsford Ltd, London

Contents

The original idea for the Portrait of a Decade series was conceived by Trevor Fisher.

Typeset by Tek-Art Ltd Kent
and printed and bound
in Great Britain by
MacLehose & Partners Ltd, Portsmouth
for the publishers
B.T. Batsford Ltd
4 Fitzhardinge Street
London W1H 0AH

ISBN 0 7134 5989 1

The frontispiece shows a Wright brothers aeroplane in flight near Le Mans in France, August 1908.

Introduction

In the unsettled years after the First World War, Europeans viewed the first decade of the twentieth century as something of a golden age. In England it was often referred to as the 'Edwardian Summer', in France as 'la Belle Epoque'. They remembered the glittering lives of the rich and well-born, which gave the era so much of its glamour and colour; the pageantry of royal weddings and funerals and the speed of technological and scientific change that made the world an exciting place in which to live.

Paris during 'la Belle Epoque': Toulouse-Lautrec's La Danse au Moulin Rouge *sums up the spirit of that age.*

A world quite different from today

The political map of Europe looked quite different then. While Britain, France, Spain and Italy were much the same shape as they are today, the central and eastern part of the continent was dominated by the three great empires of Germany, Austria-Hungary and Russia, each of whom ruled over subject peoples of many different nationalities. Distrustful of each other, the Great Powers of Europe had banded together in a system of defensive alliances. To guard against attack by France or Russia, Germany, Austria-Hungary and Italy had formed the Triple Alliance. In retaliation, France and Russia had joined together in the Dual Entente.

The Great Powers of Europe also ruled much of the rest of the world between them. Most of Africa and the Pacific and much of Asia had been absorbed into their colonial empires. Proud countries like China and Persia, while remaining nominally independent, frequently had to bow before superior European might. Furthermore, few Europeans doubted that the white races had both a right and a duty to rule and guide the 'backward' peoples of the earth – a feeling immortalized by the English poet Rudyard Kipling in 1899, in his poem *The White Man's Burden*.

First among the great nations was Britain, whose Empire covered a quarter of the globe on which her proud citizens boasted that the 'sun never set'. With a headstart in the Industrial Revolution, she had been the 'workshop of the world' since the 1850s, and for a long time her economic supremacy seemed unchallenged. In 'splendid isolation' she stood aloof from the European alliance system, for the Royal Navy, many times larger than that of her nearest rival, ruled the waves and protected both motherland and Empire

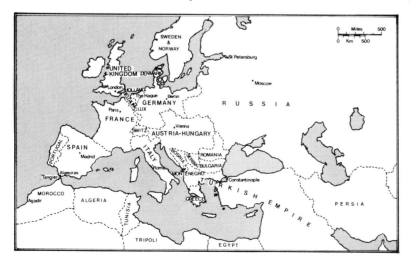

The European powers in 1900.

3

Introduction

from invasion. The celebrations for Queen Victoria's Diamond Jubilee in 1897 saw a nation at the height of its confidence and pride.

France and the United States of America were republics, with governments elected by universal male suffrage, Britain a constitutional monarchy where power mostly rested with a Parliament that was only partly democratic. Elsewhere kings and princes still ruled in fact as well as name. Where parliaments existed, as they did in Germany and Austria, they had few powers. The family relationships among the royal houses of Europe still affected politics and royal weddings and funerals were not just social events. Even in Britain, a handful of top families tended to dominate affairs and the House of Lords, with its hereditary peers, still had considerable influence.

A changing world

Despite appearances, however, by 1900 many things were changing. With their superior manpower and resources, the economies of Germany and the USA were fast overtaking the British one. The subject peoples of the Russian and Austrian Empires, who had long been restless, were getting harder to control. Czechs, Slavs, Poles and dozens of smaller ethnic groups wanted their own national states. Already the great Turkish, or Ottoman, Empire, which once stretched from the Danube to the Persian Gulf, had been shorn of most of its European territories. In South Africa the Boers challenged British rule and her overwhelming confidence began to die. In Asia too, nationalist movements were emerging that were to lead to the great independence battles of the 1940s and 1950s. Furthermore, Europe's world domination was soon to be challenged by two rising nations – the United States and Japan. The USA had recently seized the Philippines and Cuba from Spain and Japan was fast becoming a major military and industrial power in her own right.

Extremes of wealth and poverty were apparent everywhere. The great industrial cities of Europe and the USA had bred horrifying slums. Wages were low. Except in Germany, where a limited system of social security had existed since 1889, the working class had no protection against loss of income due to illness, unemployment or old age and lived in constant fear of destitution. The poor, though, were less inclined than they had been previously to accept their fate with resignation. For a long time organizations had been springing up to campaign for a better future. Trade unions used the collective strength of their members to wrest better pay and conditions from employers. Women too demanded an end to second-class status. In the nineteenth century the German Karl Marx had taught that the working class could bring down the capitalist system and replace it with a socialist society of equality and abundance. Now Socialist parties all over Europe put up candidates for parliaments and dreamed of class war and revolution. Russia, where Tsar Nicholas II held out doggedly against any form of change, came close to total collapse in 1905. With periodic bombing campaigns that they hoped would bring society to its knees, a handful of anarchists struck fear into the hearts of the privileged classes.

Some far-seeing people preached that the old order must adapt to the new age or go under, while others showed a grim determination to defend their way of life to the last ditch.

Boer commandos manning the trenches outside Mafeking. The Boer War did much to shake Britain's confidence in her own Imperial supremacy.

Introduction

A technological innovation

The mood was more optimistic when it came to the exciting new advances in science and technology. Few people questioned the belief that scientific progress was good in itself and would add to the sum of human happiness. Inventions such as the telephone, the wireless and the internal combustion engine had been developed during the last years of the nineteenth century, and in the first decade of the twentieth they began to transform the surface of society into something that would not be too unfamiliar today. Each year saw the development of new technological marvels great and small – from the aeroplane to the vacuum cleaner and the electric train to the first plastics. In the field of medicine and the physical sciences discoveries were made whose full impact would not be felt for another generation – for good or for ill. In the same few years Einstein, Rutherford and the Curies laid the groundwork for the nuclear science of the future, while the first steps were also being taken that would lead to the development of vaccines against whooping cough and diphtheria.

A decade of technological marvels: an early telephone.

Revolution in the arts

There was much that was stimulating, disturbing or shocking in the arts. Experimental artists like Picasso, Schoenberg and Frank Lloyd Wright laid the foundations of the modern movements in art, music and architecture. Many writers fell under the influence of Freud's new vision of man as the victim of his subconscious, while others, like the Russian Maxim Gorky, the Anglo-Irish Bernard Shaw and the American Upton Sinclair set out to uncover the evils of their time and transform society for the better through their writing.

Popular culture was also changing. By the end of the decade the music hall was on the verge of being pushed out by the cinema as the chief source of cheap entertainment. Most European countries now had a system of state primary education and most people could read. On the whole, what they read were not works of literature that are remembered today but romantic novelists like Elinor Glyn, adventure stories like those of A.E.W. Mason and 'gossipy' magazines like *Tit-bits*. Randolph Hearst in the United States and Alfred Harmsworth in Britain saw that the market was ready for a new kind of newspaper geared to a mass readership and the popular press was born. By 1910 sales of the *Daily Mail* and *Daily Mirror* in Britain far outstripped those of *The Times* or the *Daily Telegraph*.

No golden age

At the time people did not see the first decade of the twentieth century as an era of calm that was shattered by the outbreak of war in 1914. That was a later myth. They saw it as a time of great turbulence and change. What the shape of the world would have been had war not come we shall never know. Things were changing rapidly and even without the impact of war the world of 1920 would have been very different from that of 1900.

War in

Old enemies collide

IN OCTOBER 1899 the long-uneasy relationship between Britain and the two Boer Republics of the Transvaal and the Orange Free State had erupted into open warfare. The Boers or Afrikaaners fought because they believed that their independence and distinctive way of life depended on it, the British because they saw Boer nationalism as a threat to their control of Southern Africa and its recently-discovered gold and diamond deposits. As the greatest imperial power of her day, Britain had confidently expected this little war against two tiny nations of farmers to be over in a few weeks.

John Bull humiliated: A French magazine gloats over Britain's inability to defeat the Boers.

The tide turns

ROBERTS AND KITCHENER saw the need for more flexible tactics. British troops became more mobile and the traditional red uniforms were replaced by khaki, which blended in with the veld. The new strategy soon paid off. Kimberley was relieved in February, and the Boer army outside Ladysmith was trapped in a narrow gorge at Paardeburg and forced to surrender. In May Mafeking was relieved. The news was received in Britain with scenes of hysterical joy. By September the chief Boer towns of Bloemfontein, Pretoria and Johannesburg were under British occupation. The aged President Kruger of the Transvaal had fled abroad, a broken man. The war, it seemed, was all but over.

Mafeking is free! . . . At 9.30 last night the announcement came that the Boers had abandoned the siege . . . London went simply wild with delight. Fleet Street, which, on ordinary nights, contains only its usual number of pedestrians, was, as if by magic, transformed into a thoroughfare crowded and jammed with an excited throng of cheering, shouting, gesticulating, happy people. Whistles were blown . . . Hawkers were on the scene with that rapidity which is only equalled by the vulture when it scents its prey. In front of the newspaper offices, the crowds became thick and impassable. The police were there, but that is all, for they were as atoms in a mighty sea.
From the *Daily Express*, 18 May

Black week

AS THE YEAR OPENED, the war was, in fact, going badly for Britain. The 14,000-strong army in South Africa had little idea of how to cope with the Boer way of fighting, in which small mounted groups would strike quickly and scatter before the slower-moving British troops could retaliate. In one humiliating week in December 1899, Britain had lost three battles and the Boers had laid siege to the towns of Ladysmith, Mafeking and Kimberley, bottling thousands of British soldiers up inside. The 'little' colonial war had turned into a nightmare. Sir Redvers Buller, the defeated commander-in-chief, who was nick-named by the press 'Sir Reverse Buller', was replaced by General Roberts, with Kitchener as second-in-command. Thousands of fresh troops set sail from Britain.

The bloodiest battle of the war

ON 23 JANUARY an attack was launched on the Boer forces besieging Ladysmith. British troops stormed an enemy strong-point on Spion Kop (Lookout Hill). The hill was captured quickly but the British now found themselves under murderous fire from Boer snipers positioned on neighbouring hills. All day they held out but at sunset withdrew, leaving behind over a thousand dead. The Boers then reoccupied the Kop and the siege went on. So greatly did the British government fear that morale at home might collapse under the weight of this latest defeat that the full news about Spion Kop was kept from the public for many weeks.

South Africa

Britain celebrates: Mafeking night in Piccadilly Circus.

But the Boers were far from defeated. They reorganized themselves into commando bands and began a guerilla war against the British army of occupation. Living off the land, they staged hit-and-run raids against British camps and communications, disappearing back into the veld before the defenders could give chase. Britain began preparations for a long war of attrition and by the end of the year she had over 100,000 troops in South Africa.

Confidence dented

THE HUMILIATIONS OF 1899 AND 1900 came as a great shock to Britons and dented their confidence. The smug belief that public schools bred men of superior intelligence and moral fibre, uniquely fitted to govern a great Empire, faltered in the face of Boer hardiness and the ineptness shown by many high-ranking British officers (a lesson pointed out by Rudyard Kipling himself). Her colonial rivals, especially France and Germany, did not conceal their glee. If the other European powers had been able to forget their quarrels long enough to unite in support of the Boers, Britain's position would have been dangerous indeed and her Empire put at risk. The years of confident and arrogant Splendid Isolation were drawing to a close.

And ye vaunted your fathomless powers, and ye vaunted your iron pride,
Ere ye fawned on the younger nations for the men who could shoot and ride!
Then ye returned to your trinkets; then ye contented yourselves
With the flanelled fools at the wicket or the muddied oafs at the goals.
Rudyard Kipling, *The Islanders*.

Ferment in China

IN 1900 CHINESE RESENTMENT against the 'foreign devils' who had humiliated them throughout the nineteenth century rose to boiling point. A secret society calling itself the 'Righteous and Harmonious Fists' vowed vengeance. In order to prepare body and soul for the coming conflict, its members practised a ritual form of boxing and were nicknamed 'Boxers' by the Western press. Their cause was backed by the Dowager Empress of China, Tz'u-hsi, who had long resented the way foreign diplomats dictated to her. In the spring of 1900 the Boxers swept through northern China towards Beijing (Peking), massacring foreigners as they went. A particular butt of their hatred were Christian missionaries and their Chinese converts. On 20 June they invaded the area of the city where Europeans lived and besieged the foreigners in their compounds.

THE PEKIN MASSACRE.

ALL WHITE MEN, WOMEN, AND CHILDREN PUT TO THE SWORD.

AWFUL STORY OF THE 6TH & 7TH JULY.

HOW OUR PEOPLE DIED FIGHTING PRINCE TUAN'S HORDES.

FULL DETAILS FROM OUR SPECIAL CORRESPONDENT.

Daily Mail *headline of 16 July which reported – erroneously – the massacre of all the Europeans in Beijing. Most of them were rescued unharmed.*

Fifty-five days at Beijing

INSIDE WERE OVER 400 European and Japanese civilians, 450 armed soldiers and over 3000 Chinese Christians who had fled there for safety. In the Roman Catholic Cathedral a short distance away a further 3000 were trapped. Supplies of food were adequate but the inmates had to endure constant shelling from Chinese artillery. Little accurate news got out and the press in Europe was full of rumours about terrible massacres which turned out to be wildly exaggerated. After 55 days the siege was lifted by an international force, a rare example of the great powers of Europe acting together for a common end. Once again, China lay at the mercy of foreigners.

Philippines in revolt

WHEN THE USA defeated Spain in the short war of 1898, Filippinos expected to be granted true independence. Instead, the USA annexed the Philippines herself, along with the Hawaiian Islands. A bitter revolt, led by Emilio Aguinaldo, broke out against the new masters. Some Americans too were uncomfortable about her new role as a colonial power, for it seemed to contradict the claims of the *Declaration of Independence* that all men were created equal.

Lies! lies! It cannot be! The wars we wage
Are Noble, and our battles still are won
By justice for us, ere we lift the gage.
We have not sold our loftiest heritage.
The proud Republic hath not stooped to cheat
And scramble in the market-place of war . . .
Ah no!
We have not fallen so.

'An Ode in Time of Hesitation' by William Vaughn Moody, published in *Atlantic Monthly*, May 1900.

German navy expands

GERMANY'S NAVY MINISTER, Admiral von Tirpitz, announced a naval building programme that would equip Germany with 38 new battleships by 1920. This was necessary, he argued, to defend Germany's coast and overseas trade against attack. The British were suspicious, for they scented a challenge to the Royal Navy's domination of the High Seas. A distinctly anti-German note began to creep into the British press.

King of Italy murdered

ON 29 JULY King Umberto of Italy was shot four times as he distributed prizes after an athletics contest near Milan. He died immediately. His assassin was a young anarchist of Italian descent, who had come all the way over from his home in New Jersey, USA, to do the deed. The King's violent death sent a shudder of apprehension through the Royal Houses of Europe.

Khaki election

IN BRITAIN, a general election was held in October, and Lord Salisbury's Conservative government, which had been in office since 1895, won a clear victory. The upturn in British fortunes in South Africa had created a mood of national patriotism, and the Conservatives cashed in on this. During the campaign they all but ignored pressing social and economic questions and swept into power on a wave of jingoism. Their main rivals, the Liberals, were divided over the war and this made them very unpopular. Over half of the ministers in the new cabinet were aristocrats, some of them Salisbury's own relations.

Our brave soldiers in South Africa expect that every voter this day will do his duty. To vote for a Liberal is to vote for the Boer.
Conservative election poster, 1900

Labour Party formed

IN 1884 the vote had been given to all male householders over 21 who paid rates. For the first time many, although not all, working men could vote. At first most of these new votes went to the Liberals, and the tiny socialist parties like the Independent Labour Party (ILP) received little support. By 1900, however, it was becoming increasingly obvious that social reform on a large scale would not happen until the working class had its own representatives in Parliament. In that year a group of trade unionists and socialists formed the Labour Representation Committee (LRC) to work for the election of MPs sympathetic to the workers' cause. Its first secretary was a Scot of humble origins, Ramsay MacDonald, and most of its funds came from trade union subscriptions. The LRC attracted little attention at first, even among the working class. In the Khaki election it managed to return only two MPs: Keir Hardie and Richard Bell.

The Liberals divided

THE CONSERVATIVE VICTORY was made all the easier because their main rivals, the Liberals, were sharply divided over the war. Prominent party leaders like H.H. Asquith supported it, while others, including the dynamic young Welshman, David Lloyd George, condemned it as a criminal waste of lives and money. Such views killed any Liberal chance of winning. When Lloyd George tried to speak against the war in Birmingham Town Hall, he was howled down by the audience and had to escape by a back exit disguised as a policeman. It seemed that a long period of Conservative rule lay ahead.

Such a war will bring you no glory. It will bring you no profit but mischief and it will be wrong. You may make thousands of women widows and thousands of children fatherless. It will be wrong. You may add a new province to your Empire and it will still be wrong.

Speech by John Morley, a Liberal, in January

Sport and the Arts

The popular press is born

THE SPREAD OF MASS LITERACY in the nineteenth century had led to the rise of the popular press – the forerunners of the modern tabloids – in the United States and Britain. By 1900, the *Daily Mail* (founded in 1896) and the *Daily Express* (1900) had far bigger circulations than the old quality dailies like *The Times* and the *Daily Telegraph*. Their articles were kept short and easy to read and were designed to excite and entertain as much as to inform. Taking advantage of the mass readership, much of their space was filled with advertisements. There were no laws laying down standards, and the claims they made were often much more brash and sweeping than would be permitted today.

The past uncovered

A BRITISH ARCHAEOLOGIST, Sir Arthur Evans, uncovered the first traces of the Palace of Knossos on Crete and provided the first firm evidence of the mysterious Minoan civilization that had flourished there between 2500 and 1100 BC.

The power of the subconscious

AN AUSTRIAN NEUROLOGIST, Sigmund Freud, published *The Interpretation of Dreams*. From his clinical experience he had concluded that much human unhappiness and even illness came from unresolved childhood conflicts that had been buried deep in the subconscious. Often these hidden problems surfaced in dreams. This was a spectacular break with the nineteenth-century faith that man was totally logical and rational and has since become a basis for modern psychoanalysis.

The father of modern psychoanalysis: Sigmund Freud.

New music
Three new works by well-known composers were first performed in 1900:
The Dream of Gerontius, an oratorio by the Englishman, Edward Elgar.
The Austrian, Gustav Mahler, wrote his fourth symphony.
Finlandia, by the Finn, Jean Sibelius.

New books for children published in 1900
The Wizard of Oz by Frank Baum.
The Tale of Peter Rabbit, by Beatrix Potter.
Little Black Sambo, by Helen Bannerman. This was highly popular at the time but is not acceptable today because of its patronizing racial attitudes.

Other sporting news

AN AMERICAN BUSINESSMAN, D.F. Davis, presented a cup to be awarded to the winner of a knock-out contest for national lawn tennis teams. Victory was to go to the winner of the best of five matches – four singles and one doubles. As the Davis Cup, it is still competed for today. In 1900 the USA beat Britain in the final.

The world's first international road race was run between Paris and Lyons. Five cars from France, Britain and the USA competed for a trophy put up by an American businessman, Gordon Bennett. The winning French car averaged a speed of 38.5 mph (62 km/h).

Olympic Games held in Paris

THE SECOND OLYMPIC GAMES of modern times were held in Paris in conjunction with the Exhibition there. The events were spread out over six months and were very badly organized. Discus throwers, for example, had to throw in a park full of trees. Of the 1300 competitors only 11 were women and some athletes refused to compete on Sundays. The star of the Games was Roy Ewing of the USA, who had been confined to a wheelchair as a child but went on to win three gold medals in the high jump.

Airship takes off

MAN'S LONG-TIME WISH to defy gravity and fly took a step nearer fulfilment when an airship named after its designer, the German Count Zepplin, completed a successful test flight over Lake Constance near the Swiss-German border. Zepplin himself was one of the five men on board. A cross between a hot-air balloon and a modern aeroplane, it had a rigid aluminium frame covered with impregnated cotton and was kept aloft by 400,000 cubic feet of hydrogen stored in seventeen gas-tight bags. Unlike a balloon, however, it was not dependent on wind and air currents to keep it up in the air or control its direction, for it was fitted with a rudder and two petrol engines. On this flight it reached a height of 1000 feet and stayed up for eighteen minutes.

The wonders of modern technology

THE PUBLIC were able to see for themselves some of the new technological marvels at the Great Paris Exhibition that ran throughout the spring and summer and which sold over 47 million entrance tickets. It was the first exhibition to be powered by electricity and visitors were able to ride on an escalator, the first in Europe, and move around the site on an electrically-powered moving platform. X-rays, wireless telegraphs, motor cars and silent movies were among the wonders on display.

The technological wonders of the age on display: the Palace of Electricity at the Paris Exhibition.

Medical breakthroughs

AN ENGLISH DOCTOR, Sir Patrick Mason, identified the mosquito as the carrier of malaria, which affected up to 10 per cent of the world's population. The disease is transmitted when an insect sucks the blood of a person infected with the malaria parasite and then bites someone else. This discovery was the crucial first step in twentieth century attempts to eradicate the disease.

Some 'firsts' of 1900

Oxy-acetylene torch, invented in France, which gave a heat of up to 3000°C and became the basis for much modern welding work.

Caterpillar tracks were invented in the USA by Benjamin Holt. These spread the load of a heavy vehicle over a much larger area than would be possible with normal wheels and enabled it to travel over soft ground without sinking in – the basis of the modern bulldozer and tank.

Brownie Box Camera was first produced in the USA by the firm of Eastman-Kodak. It was the world's first really simple camera and remained popular for decades.

The first fully-automated telephone exchange came into operation in Massachusetts, carrying 10,000 lines that could work at a distance of up to a mile. To connect a caller, an idle line was selected by a motor-driven interceptor. A ringing tone was then heard by both caller and called. When the receiver on one end was replaced, the connection was then automatically broken because both lines were earthed.

End of an era:

A new century begins

THE YEAR 1901, rather than 1900, had been officially proclaimed as the beginning of the new century and so a sense of excitement and anticipation was in the air.

The twentieth century has dawned on us; and as we float past this great landmark on the shores of time, feelings of awe and wonder naturally creep over us... What will be the history of mankind in the hundred years whose first hours are even now gliding by? What changes will the new century witness? Will they be mainly for good or for evil? Will the dominance of man over nature increase in the same degree or to a far greater degree than in the age gone by? How the changes will affect the morals and minds of men remains a subject for speculation. Will they be healthier, longer-lived, better and more intelligent, or will they remain much the same as the people we have known?

The Times, 1 January

Symbol of an era

THREE WEEKS into the new century, on 22 January, Queen Victoria died at Osborne House on the Isle of Wight. In a way she had been a symbol of the age that had just passed. She was 82 years old, had reigned for 63 years and had given her name to an era of history in which Britain had become the world's greatest power. To be British was something to be proud of.

La Reyne est Morte (The Queen is Dead)
God help our England, for we stand
Orphaned of her who made us one;
The Honour of the Fatherland,
Her hope, her trust, her Sun

. . . . .

The scattered islands of Her Realm
Shall drop the emblem of her sway
Who through the long years steered the helm –
Through the laborious day.

And flashing lights shall signal far
Their tidings to passing ships
To tell the sinking of her Star,
Her sorrowful eclipse
From *The Times*, 23 January

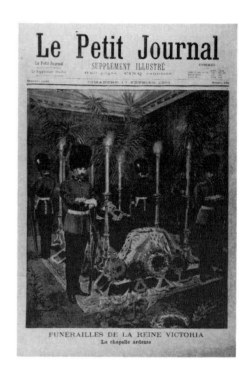

Le Petit Journal
SUPPLEMENT ILLUSTRÉ

FUNERAILLES DE LA REINE VICTORIA
La chapelle ardente

A French magazine pays tribute to the passing of Queen Victoria, which many saw as the passing of an age.

The first 5 ranks of Queen Victoria's funeral cortege, published in the *Daily Express*		
HRH The Duke of Connaught	THE KING	HIM The German Emperor
HM The King of the Hellenes		HM The King of Portugal
HRH Prince Henry of Prussia	HRH Prince Christian of Schleswig-Holstein	HRH The Grand Duke of Hesse
HRH The Crown Prince of Rumania	HI and RH The Crown Prince of Germany	HRH The Duke of Sparta
HRH The Crown Prince of Sweden and Norway	HI and RH The Archduke Francis Ferdinand of Austria	HRH The Hereditary Grand Duke Michael of Russia

The Crowned Heads gather

THE QUEEN, who had had nine children and 39 grandchildren, was related to most of the royalty of Europe. The Kaiser (Emperor) Wilhelm II of Germany was a grandson and the Tsarina Alexandra of Russia a granddaughter. The close relatives who followed the funeral cortege on its way through London to Paddington Station

Queen Victoria dies

The grandmother of Europe is buried. Edward VII (right) and Kaiser Wilhelm II of Germany head Queen Victoria's funeral procession.

for the burial at Windsor contained four reigning Kings and four heirs apparent. In spite of the sense that things were changing, no one suspected that this was one of the last times that the ruling class of Europe would gather together before many of them were swept away by the First World War.

The new King

THE NEW KING, Edward VII, was nearly 60 years old and had lived all his life in the shadow of his mother, who had allowed him to take little responsibility for affairs of state. In contrast to Victoria's rather stodgy respectability, he was something of a libertine with a great love of women, brandy, cigars and racehorses. He was also cosmopolitan and gregarious, a good judge of character and very shrewd. Certainly the tone of the new reign would be very different from that of the old.

The end of an era?

OTHER THINGS WERE CHANGING TOO, for cracks were appearing in that self-confidence and sense of superiority that had been the hallmark of Victorian Britain. The humiliation in South Africa was one reason for this but so too was the sense that the world was changing fast and that the old certainties would no longer hold true. To many the death of the old Queen was like the end of an era.

Queen Victoria's death alone will ever mark 1901 in the history of the nation. With her departed, perhaps, the most glorious era of English history. The end of the Boer War, which was confidently assumed with the fall of Pretoria, is not yet . . . Trade has only been fair. We are on the eve of great electrification movements. The automobile has come to stay, and there are even some people who predict that in another generation our traffic will be horseless. . . women are coming more and more into competition with men in business, and even well-to-do girls are devoting themselves to callings other than nursing.
From the diary of R.D. Blumenfeld, an English journalist

It was impossible not to sense, in that stately procession, the passing of an epoch, and a great one; a period in which England had been supreme, and had attained to the height of her material wealth and power. There were many who wondered, doubted perhaps, whether that greatness would continue; who read in the failures of the early part of the Boer War a sign of decadence, and influenced perhaps unduly, by Gibbons' *Decline and Fall* . . . I felt I was witnessing the funeral procession of England's greatness and glory.
From the diary of Elinor Glyn, a popular writer of romantic fiction.

American president assassinated

ON 14 SEPTEMBER President McKinley of the United States, who had just been re-elected for a second term, was assassinated by an anarchist in Buffalo. He was the third US President to be shot whilst in office in the past 40 years. His successor, Vice-President Theodore 'Teddy' Roosevelt, was a man of extraordinary physical and mental energy and an unashamed believer in the right of the American people to dominate the continent, both north and south. During the Spanish-American War he had raised his own cavalry regiment, the Rough Riders, and had led a famous and successful charge to capture San Juan Hill in Cuba. Many Americans admired him greatly, but others thought he was little more than a 'cowboy' who would lead the US into all sorts of dangerous foreign adventures.

'Britain finds that the concentration camps aren't such a good idea after all.'

Philippines conquered

THE REBELLION IN THE PHILIPPINES was finally suppressed in 1901. It had cost far more American lives than the Spanish war itself and damaged her reputation as the Land of the Free. But the United States was now firmly established as a Pacific power to be reckoned with.

The war goes on

WAR IN SOUTH AFRICA dragged on. Although a further 100,000 British troops poured in during 1901, the Boer commandos, who never numbered more than about 30,000, proved just how difficult it can be to defeat a guerilla force who have the sympathy of the local population. In desperation, Kitchener, who was now in charge, began a 'scorched earth' policy. The countryside was divided into sectors by means of a chain of 'blockhouses' joined together by wire fences. Each area could then be systematically searched and its farms and crops burnt. The homeless civilians – mostly women, children and the old – were then herded into 'concentration' camps, where the army was supposed to look after them. Through mismanagement rather than design, the camps were swept by epidemics. Over 20,000 Boers, most of them children, died of measles, pneumonia and enteric fever. When the news leaked out, public opinion both in Britain and the rest of the world was outraged. The Liberal leader, Campbell Bannerman, called the camps 'methods of barbarism'. And still the Boers fought on.

A new nation: Australia

ON 1 JANUARY the six separate colonies on the Australian continent, with a total population of four and a half millions, became a nation in their own right, when they united to form the Commonwealth of Australia and were granted self-government or 'Dominion' status by Britain. The new state adopted a federal system of government, similar to the American one, in which the individual states retained great power over their internal affairs. A new Federal capital was built at Canberra, carefully chosen to be equidistant from most of the main cities of eastern Australia.

The creation of the Commonwealth of Australia continued a British tradition that had begun with Canada in 1867 of giving self-government to the all-white colonies, although there was still no thought of doing the same for the non-white ones. From the beginning the new nation expressed her determination to follow a 'White Australia' policy and to restrict the immigration of coloured people.

Poverty widespread in Britain

A STUDY OF THE LIVES of the working class in York caused a shock. Seebohm Rowntree's *Poverty, a Study in Town Life* revealed that 30 per cent of the town's inhabitants lived below the poverty line and barely earned enough to survive. At the same time recruits for the Boer War were being rejected by the thousands as unfit for active service, mainly as a result of early malnutrition or untreated childhood diseases. The implications of this for Britain's future worried many.

That in this land of abounding wealth, during a time of perhaps unexampled prosperity, probably more than one fourth of the population are living in poverty, is a fact which may well cause great searchings of the heart. There is surely need for a greater concentration of thought by the nation upon the well-being of its people, for no civilization can be sound or stable which has as its base this mass of stunted human life. The suffering may be all but voiceless, and we may long remain ignorant of its extent and severity, but when once we realise it we see that social questions of profound importance await solution.
From S. Rowntree, *Poverty, a Study in Town Life*

Poverty alongside affluence: unemployed men begging in a London street.

Trade Unionism under fire

1901 WAS A BAD YEAR for British trade unions. The Taff Vale Railway Company in South Wales sued the railwaymen's union for losses the company had suffered during a strike in 1900. The House of Lords, before whom the case eventually came, ruled that henceforth all unions should be held liable for the damage caused by strikes. The railwaymen themselves were forced to pay up £23,000. A wave of shock went through the whole trade union movement, for striking could now become so cripplingly expensive that no union would be able to afford it. Only Parliament could reverse this decision. As working men realized this, membership of the LRC, which had grown only slowly in 1900, shot up.

An architectural revolution begins

IN THE MID-NINETEENTH CENTURY iron and steel frames were developed that were strong enough to bear the weight of a building. Since the walls would no longer have to carry the full load, they could be built of lighter materials like glass. In 1901 the American, Frank Lloyd Wright published a pamphlet in which he argued that modern materials made it possible to make maximum use of space and light, and in future the beauty of a building would be judged by the way it made use of these natural assets. Both the style and the materials should be kept as simple and functional as possible and should blend in with their surroundings. These principles should be applied to all buildings, whether public or private, large or small. Such ideas were the forerunners of modern architecture, although some people would argue that much modern design falls far short of the ideal. Frank Lloyd Wright himself went on to become famous for the design of the first open-plan houses.

The building of the future will be simplified and etherealised. In it space is more spacious, and the sense of it may enter into every building, great or small.
The Art and Craft of the Machine, by Frank Lloyd Wright, 1901

New plays

ONE OF THE THEATRICAL FASHIONS of the time was 'naturalism'. Plays should not over-dramatize but show life as it really is in all its subtlety. They should no longer be divided into comedy and tragedy, for real life is a mixture of both. Actors were taught to make the most of every pause and change of tone and not to rely on theatrical histrionics for effect. Two new plays by masters of the naturalist drama that were put on in 1901, were *Three Sisters*, by Anton Chekhov which was put on by the Moscow Art Theatre and *Dance of Death*, by the Swede, August Strindberg, which shows scenes from an unhappy marriage.

A new popular sport

AT THIS TIME most sportsmen were still amateurs and proud to be so. In Britain, in particular, playing the game in the right spirit was still considered more important than winning. The exception was Association football or soccer, where the professional teams of the Football League (founded in 1887) attracted huge crowds and were fast becoming Britain's most popular winter spectator sport. In 1901 the League had two divisions, containing 36 teams in all. All of them, except Woolwich Arsenal, came from the Midlands and the North. Among the most successful teams of the time were Aston Villa, Newcastle United, Sunderland and Sheffield Wednesday. In 1901 110,000 people watched the FA Cup Final at Crystal Palace, in which Spurs of the Southern League and Sheffield Utd. of Division I drew 2-2. Spurs won the replay 3-1 and became the only non-League side ever to win the Cup. Abroad the English national side had as yet no serious rivals. In 1901 she played two internationals against a German side and won 12-0 and 10-0.

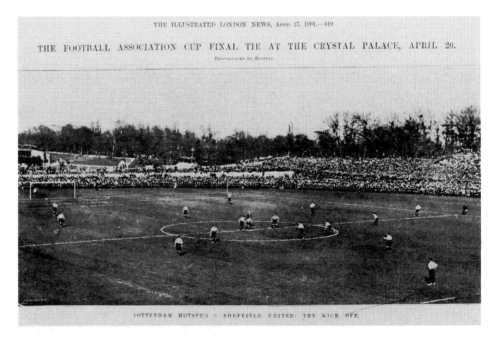

Britain's most popular spectator sport. The 1901 Cup Final at Crystal Palace.

New music
Three still-famous musical works were first performed in 1901:
Piano Concerto No.1 by Rachmaninov
Symphony No.2 in D by Sibelius
Pomp and Circumstance Marches Nos.1 and 2 by Edward Elgar. In 1902 the first of these marches was set to the words of 'Land of Hope and Glory'.

Wireless breakthrough

WHEN THE TWENTIETH CENTURY OPENED, it was already possible to send messages across the Atlantic by cable telegraph. But cables were hard to install, easy to cut in wartime and broke down frequently. Messages sent by radio or 'wireless', on the other hand, would make uninterrupted trans-Atlantic communication possible, also making it possible to contact ships at sea. On 12 December 1901 a young Italian, Guglielmo Marconi, managed to transmit the three dots of the letter 'S' 1800 miles from Goonhilly Down in Cornwall to Newfoundland on the east coast of Canada. That such a thing was possible surprised scientists, because all waves – both light and radio – travel on a straight line, and Marconi's message should have flown off into space. The explanation was only found in 1924, when the existence of the ionisphere, which bounces radio waves back to earth, was discovered.

Some medical breakthroughs

KARL LANDSTEINER at the Institute of Hygiene in Vienna discovered that human blood was divided into three incompatible groups, which he called A, B, and O (the AB group was discovered two years later). The way was now open to safer blood transfusions.

A German bacteriologist, Emil van Behring, received the Nobel Prize for his work on diphtheria. He had infected animals with the disease and extracted the antibodies from their blood serum. When injected into humans, these antibodies should then confer lifelong immunity. Serum therapy promised an end to a disease that killed over 10,000 children every year in Britain, but its use did not become widespread until after the Second World War.

Some 'firsts' in 1901

The vacuum cleaner, invented by an English engineer, Hubert Cecil Booth. This early version was too large to go inside a building. It was driven around on a horse-drawn cart and the four suction hoses, each one hundred feet long, were passed through windows. Booth's firm, The Vacuum Cleaner Company, were given the contract to clean the carpet in Westminster Abbey for Edward VII's coronation in 1902.

Safety razor A new type of razor went on sale in the United States, to replace the dangerous *cut-throat razor* which had been used up to then. The blade was fixed inside a guard so that only the very edge was left bare and could pass over the skin without cutting it. The blades were disposable and no longer had to be sharpened. This is the type of razor still used today. Its inventor was King C. Gillette.

Finger-print file, which made the identification of criminals easier, was installed at Scotland Yard. The first conviction in which finger-print evidence played a crucial part was in 1905.

Electricity arrives

THE PRINCIPLES OF ELECTRICITY and its use for lighting and heating were well-known by 1901. High voltage power was first generated by power stations and then transformed down to 240 (Britain) or 120 (USA) volts for local use. There were two and a half million electric street lamps in London by 1901, and 10 per cent of urban homes in the USA had electric light. Electricity, though, had little impact on the lives of poor people or those living in rural areas and was still only available to the rich.

Electric street lighting in London.

The great

A MAN OF HIS WORD.

Russian Bear still in Manchuria). "I SAID I'D GO, AND—HERE I AM!"

The scheming Russian bear: Punch, *like most Britons, was convinced that Russia had designs on Manchuria and the rest of the Far East.*

The Russian bear

FOR MANY YEARS other nations had watched Russia's activities in the Far East with suspicion and distrust. During the nineteenth century her frontiers had expanded eastwards to the Pacific and southwards to the borders of China and Afghanistan. Perhaps her eyes were now on Korea or Manchuria or even China herself! Japan, who had her own ambitions in these areas, was suspicious. So too was Britain, who was worried about the security of India's North-West Frontier and about her trade with China. And if it came to war in the Far East, then France, Russia's ally, might be tempted to join in and snatch British colonies there. The prospects were alarming indeed.

The rising sun

SINCE THE MIDDLE of the last century, Japan had transformed herself from a society on the fringes of world politics into a military and industrial power to be reckoned with. Her navy of six modern battleships and six armoured cruisers was British-built and trained and her army modelled on that of Germany. She had even sent observers to the Franco-Prussian War in 1870 to learn what they could of the latest military techniques. And Japan had a grudge, for in 1894-5 she had defeated China and seized the valuable ice-free harbour of Port Arthur on the Liaotung Peninsula. Russia had ordered her to give it up, and not yet willing to challenge Russia outright, Japan had complied. Now the Russians held Port Arthur but the Japanese had not forgotten the incident.

Russian scare

An unlikely alliance

ON 30 JANUARY Britain signed a treaty of alliance with Japan, the first alliance she had made since those of the Napoleonic Wars a century before, making the first break with the policy of Splendid Isolation. It was the first treaty ever to be signed between a European and Asiatic country on terms of absolute equality and was designed to ensure that in a future war between Russia and Japan, France would not dare to come to her ally's aid, for if she did Britain would come to Japan's. Britain's possessions in the Far East would thus be safe from French attack and part of her Pacific fleet freed for duties elsewhere.

Art. I The High Contracting Parties, having mutually recognised the independence of China and Korea, declare themselves to be entirely uninfluenced by any aggressive tendencies in either country. Having in view, however, their special interests . . . the High Contracting Parties recognise that it will be admissible for either of them to take such measures as may be indispensable in order to safeguard those interests if threatened either by the aggressive action of any other Power, or by disturbances arising in China or Korea. . .
Art. II If either Great Britain or Japan, in the defence of their interests, should become involved in a war with another Power, the other High Contracting Party will maintain a strict neutrality, and use its efforts to prevent other Powers from joining in hostilities against its ally.
Art. III If, in the above event, any other Power or Powers should join in hostilities against that ally, the other High Contracting Party will come to its assistance, and will conduct the war in common. . .
Part of the Anglo-Japanese Treaty, published 11 February 1902

A continent crossed

IN MAY Russia's new Trans-Siberian Railway reached Vladivostok on the Pacific. It was 5778 miles long (9297 km) and had taken ten years to build. It was a fairly primitive single-track railway, where in some places trains could go no faster than 15 mph (24 km/h). There was still an unfinished stretch around Lake Baikal, where passengers had to disembark and cross the lake by ferry, but it cut the journey from Moscow to the Far East down to about a fortnight and did nothing to calm British and Japanese suspicions of Russia's designs there.

The Great Game goes on

FOR A LONG TIME BRITAIN HAD employed secret agents whose job it was to spy out Russian activities in Afghanistan, Persia or Nepal and report anything suspicious. This was known as 'playing the Great Game'. In 1902 rumours began to circulate that a Russian agent, Dorigev, was plotting in Lhasa, the Tibetan capital, to bring that country, which lay so near to the Indian frontier, into the Russian sphere of influence. Alarmed, Lord Curzon, the Viceroy of India, begged London for permission to send an armed expedition to 'persuade' Tibet's ruler, the Dalai Lama, not to become too friendly with the Russians. London hesitated but Curzon was insistent, and by the end of the year an expeditionary force was getting ready in India to move into the unknown remoteness of Tibet.

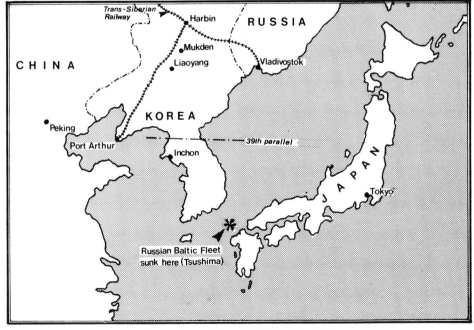

A world troublespot: the Far East 1902.

World News

Russian Minister assassinated

St Petersburg, April 15
(From our correspondent)
M. Sipyagin was on his way to attend a meeting of the Council of Ministers when he was shot. He had just entered the Imperial Council Office when a man in the uniform of an officer, who shortly before had driven up in a carriage and was awaiting the minister's arrival, advanced towards M. Sipyagin and handed him a document, at the same time remarking that he had been empowered by the Grand Duke Sergei to hand the paper to him. As M. Sipyagin took the document, the supposed officer fired five shots at him from a revolver. Two of them inflicted mortal wounds. . . The assassin, who offered no resistance, was immediately arrested.
The Times, 16 April

The Russian Minister of the Interior's

assassin was a member of a new underground revolutionary group, the Socialist Revolutionaries, who believed in assassination as a revolutionary weapon, in view of the Tsar Nicholas II's refusal to grant the most basic civil or political rights to his people.

Terrorist activity, consisting in destroying the most harmful person in the government, aims to undermine the prestige of the government and arouse in this manner the revolutionary spirit of the people and their confidence in the success of the cause.
From the Programme of the Socialist Revolutionary Party, founded in 1902

Cuba becomes a Republic

US TROOPS, who had occupied Cuba since the end of the war with Spain, left and the island became a Republic. Before they went, however, Roosevelt had insisted on a clause being inserted into the new constitution giving the US the right to establish naval bases there and intervene if necessary to preserve law and order and protect US business interests. Those who knew the President never doubted that this limitation on Cuban independence was very real. The USA still has a naval base at Guantanamo Bay today.

The funeral of Sipyagin in St Petersburg, 17 April.

The USA takes up the 'white man's burden'. Teddy Roosevelt was sure of America's right to power and influence over smaller nations.

Education Act causes controversy

ALTHOUGH ENGLAND AND WALES had had a nationwide system of free elementary schools for five to 12 year-olds since 1870, the quality of these schools varied widely from area to area. There was so little provision for state secondary education, that many people saw this as one of the reasons why England was falling behind her industrial rivals like Germany. Balfour (who had just succeeded his uncle Lord Salisbury as Prime Minister) and the government tried to remedy this situation. In areas where the only elementary school was run by the Church of England, a grant was to be given to bring that school up to an acceptable standard. Local authorities were also given permission to set up secondary or grammar schools for able children over 12, although these didn't have to be free. The 1902 Education Act caused a storm of indignation. Some critics accused the government of missing a golden opportunity to set up a comprehensive national system of secondary education. The Non-Conformists, on the other hand, objected to the public subsidy of church schools, especially if their children were forced to attend one. 'Religion on the rates' became the battle-cry. The Conservative government's popularity sank.

Elections in France

NINETY PER CENT of the electorate voted in the French general election in August. The main issue at stake was the future of the Roman Catholic Church, which many Frenchmen believed meddled too much in politics and was in league with monarchists in undermining the Republic. The election result was an overwhelming victory for the anti-clerical Bloc Republican, who wanted strong laws which would confine the Church to purely religious matters. The violently anti-clerical Emile Combes became Prime Minister.

Boer War ends

BY THE BEGINNING OF 1902 both sides were weary of the war. For Britain, it had been expensive and humiliating, and still the enemy fought on. For their part, the Boers realized that however long they held out they could not win. Meanwhile their families were suffering and their lands being ravaged. The peace treaty that was signed at Vereeniging in May was lenient. The Transvaal and Orange Free State were annexed by Britain but eventual self-government promised. The Afrikaans language and culture were to be protected and black South Africans excluded from politics. Funds were made available to rebuild farms. The Boers, it was claimed, had 'lost the war but won the peace'.

Australian women get the vote

AUSTRALIA became only the second country in the world, after New Zealand, to give the vote to women in national elections.

Coronation postponed

THE CORONATION OF KING EDWARD VII was postponed when the King fell suddenly ill with appendicitis. For a few days his life hung in the balance but by August he had recovered. The rescheduled coronation was a quiet affair, not the glittering event of the decade that had originally been planned.

Sport and the Arts

Revolutionary play staged

THEATRICAL REALISM reached a climax when the Moscow Art Theatre put on a performance of Maxim Gorky's *The Lower Depths*, a play about down and outs in a doss house. Gorky had close contacts with revolutionary groups in Russia, especially with Lenin and his followers, and saw drama as a way of changing society. The criminals and social misfits he portrays have sunk to the bottom of society because poverty and injustice have driven them there. Gorky was a forerunner of the Russian 'proletarian' writers of the 1920s.

Realism in the theatre: the doss house scene from the opening production of Gorky's The Lower Depths *in Moscow.*

Imperialism under fire

IMPERIALISM and the right of the white races to rule the earth was seldom questioned by Europeans at this time, but it came under heavy fire in a book published in 1902. In *Imperialism: A Study* J.A. Hobson argued that empires, especially the British one, brought no benefits at all to the native peoples and few to most whites. They only benefited the great business powers who were the real force behind European governments. Unable to find sufficient outlet for their products at home, they saw colonies as ready-made markets and colonial wars as sources of profit. Ordinary workers on the other hand, gained nothing. Hobson's ideas were later taken up by left-wing writers like Lenin, and sowed the seeds of doubt about the morality of Imperialism widely.

Although the new Imperialism has been bad business for the nation, it has been good business for certain classes and certain trades within the nations. The vast expenditure on armaments, the costly wars, the grave risks and embarrassments of foreign policy, the stoppage of political and social reforms within Great Britain, though **fraught with grave injury for the nation, have served well the present business interests of certain industries and professions.**
From *Imperialism: A Study* by J.A. Hobson, 1902

Some Popular British Novels and Poetry published in 1902
The Hound of the Baskervilles, by Arthur Conan Doyle, the most famous of the Sherlock Holmes stories.
Just So Stories and *Kim* by Rudyard Kipling, which drew their inspiration from Indian culture and the British experience there.
The Four Feathers, by A.E.W. Mason, a popular tale of a soldier accused of cowardice who sets out to redeem his reputation. Set in the Sudan.
Salt Water Ballads, by John Masefield, which included the famous poem beginning 'I must down to the seas again'.
Youth, by Joseph Conrad, a classic sea story by a Pole who became a master of the English language. He also wrote *Lord Jim* (1900).

Immortality for Caruso

THE ITALIAN, Enrico Caruso, who specialized in singing roles from the great Italian and French operas, was the most famous opera star of his day. In 1902 he was also the first to immortalize his voice on the new gramophone records. Among these early recordings were songs from *Rigoletto* and *Aida* by Verdi, *Tosca* by Puccini and *The Pearl Fishers* by Bizet.

20 die as football stand collapses

BRITAIN'S WORST SPORTING DISASTER occurred at Ibrox Park in Glasgow during the England v. Scotland international on 5 April. With 70,000 spectators crammed into the ground, a stand collapsed. Twenty people died and 200 were badly injured, some as they plunged 50 feet to the ground and others trampled underfoot in the ensuing panic.

Radium isolated

THE HUSBAND AND WIFE TEAM of Pierre and Marie Curie announced to the world that they had discovered a new, highly radioactive element – radium. This breakthrough was the result of four years of exhausting and often disheartening work trying to isolate enough radium from pitchblende to prove their case beyond doubt. Scorned by other scientists, they had to buy all their raw materials themselves and work through all seasons in an unheated shed. Now, however, Marie Curie was able to hold up one gram of pure radium, glowing with the blue phosphorescence that is the sign of intense radioactivity. This discovery was one of the bases of modern nuclear research and of radiography as a cancer treatment.

The Curies at work in their shed.

Better motoring

EARLY MOTOR CARS were rather primitive affairs. Three inventions in 1902 helped to make them safer and more efficient. A Belgian firm marketed the first car with an electric starting system instead of a crank handle, and in France the Renault company produced the first drum brake. When the driver pressed the brake pedal, two shoes were pushed outwards against a rotating drum fixed to the inside of the wheel and locked them. This is still the type of rear brake fitted to most modern passenger cars. Previously the valves which let petrol and air into the pistons of a car's engine and let out the waste gases had been atmosperhically-operated. This was rather a hit and miss system and gave an erratic engine performance. In 1902 Mercedes and Lanchester cars were fitted for the first time with electrically-operated valves of the type still used today.

Aswam dam opened

EVERY AUTUMN the River Nile in Egypt overflowed its banks, flooding the fertile farmland on either side. At the same time, other land, only a short distance away, was permanently arid and useless. In 1902 a dam was opened on the river to control the flow of water all the year round and prevent the annual flood. The stored water could then be used in irrigation projects over a wide area. The dam was regarded as one of the technological wonders of the age.

Looking northwards, what struck me was the shrinkage of the river. It was no longer a broad sweeping stream . . . the river is broken up into minor streams, which as the sluices opened belched forth in a cascade of white foam. There are 180 of these sluices. I should like to be there when they are all opened at the same time. . . . For centuries, it may be for ages, the dam of Aswam will remain an imperishable monument to English rule. With that knowledge we can rest content.
The Times, 20 December, whose correspondent was at the opening ceremony

Hormones discovered

TWO BRITISH SCIENTISTS, William Bayliss and Ernest Starling, discovered the presence of a substance called secretin in the human body. Its job was to stimulate the production of digestive juices after meals, and the name 'hormone' – from the Greek meaning 'to rouse to activity' – was invented to describe its effect. This was the first in a long line of hormones discovered during the twentieth century, which have improved our understanding of how the human body works and opened the way to the treatment of hormone-deficiency diseases like diabetes and thyroid deficiency (cretinism). The study of hormones and their effects is called endocrinology.

Queen uses electronic hearing aid

AT HER HUSBAND'S CORONATION, Queen Alexandra, who was very deaf, used the world's first electronic hearing aid. It had to be plugged in at the mains and weighed over 16 lbs.

1903 Entente

Old enemies

RELATIONS BETWEEN BRITAIN and her neighbour France had been tense during the closing years of the nineteenth century. Colonial disputes were at the root of this hostility, and the two nations had almost gone to war in 1898 over an incident at Fashoda in the Sudan. That France was an ally of Russia, Britain's rival in the Far East, was a further cause of contention. It was the German conviction – which seemed reasonable on the surface – that Britain would never make friends with either France or Russia that gave her the confidence to go ahead with her provocative naval programme.

Mending fences

BENEATH THE SURFACE, though, attitudes were changing. Intelligent French politicians like Foreign Minister Theophile Delcassé did not really want to run the risks of war with Britain, and he was worried by the build-up of German arms and the Kaiser's militaristic language. Certainly an Anglo-German alliance, which did not seem unlikely to many at the time, must be avoided at all costs. Britain also had reasons for mending her fences with France. The Boer War had shown the dangers of being on bad terms with *everyone*, and the German naval build-up was causing disquiet. It only needed someone to break the ice.

The personal touch

EDWARD VII was a Francophile, who was also eager to play an active role in public affairs. In the spring of 1903 he embarked on a Mediterranean tour, visiting royal relatives in Portugal, Spain and Italy. On his own initiative, he suggested that a visit to Paris on the way home might help to thaw Anglo-French relations but until the last moment, most people doubted whether such a visit would actually go ahead.

The King in Paris

THE KING'S SPECIAL TRAIN arrived at a small station in the Bois de Boulogne near Paris at 2.55 on the afternoon of 1 May. The route into Paris itself was lined with thousands of curious onlookers. There was much hostility and booing and some of the King's entourage felt very uncomfortable. Edward himself set out to be at his most charming. For four days, in between the inevitable official functions, he threw himself into the life of the capital. He saw a play at the Comédie-Française (a lively and frivolous one, at the King's own request) and insisted on meeting the actresses afterwards. He called in at the Town Hall to drink champagne with the President of the City Council and went to the races at Longchamps.

I shall never forget my visit to your charming city. I have known Paris since my childhood. I have returned here many times and I have always admired the beauty of this unique city and *esprit* [spirit] of its inhabitants. I do assure you that it is with the greatest pleasure that I find myself among you again here, where I shall always feel just as though I am at home.
From Edward VII's speech at Paris Town Hall, 2 May

Paris won over

BY THE TIME HE DEPARTED, the people of Paris had been won over. He was driven back to the station on the 4 May through crowds shouting 'Vive le Roi' and 'Vive L'Angleterre'. The way had been eased for warmer Franco-British relations, which the French press dubbed the 'Entente Cordiale'.

Si nous n'amions guère
Tes mufles d'sujets
Edouard, mon vieux frère
Toi, tu nous allais

Though there's little joy
From your people's spite
Edward, old boy,
You, you're alright
From a French song, popular in Paris, May 1903

Cordiale

Winning Paris over by his charm, Edward VII escorts Mme Loubet, the President's wife, into dinner.

An Englishman in plus-fours and a Frenchman in a velvet coat swop hats and stand beneath each other's flags in this French cartoon tribute to the Entente Cordiale.

Return visit

IN JULY President Loubet of France paid a return visit, which was very nearly wrecked before it began over a matter of protocol. It was customary for those being received at the Palace to wear knee-breeches. Loubet refused. As the President of a Republic, he would not wear such symbols of aristocratic privilege. He would wear trousers instead, as American visitors had always been allowed to do. Normally a stickler for protocol, Edward gave way this time and the visit went ahead without a hitch.

Down to business

THIS TIME Delcassé was also a member of the party and serious talks went on behind the scenes. By the end of July the outline of an agreement had been drawn up, in which the two nations patched up their colonial quarrels. In return for a French surrender of her claims to Egypt – the biggest concession of them all – Britain promised France a free hand in Morocco, where the Sultan was commonly believed to be on the point of losing control. Nothing was actually signed, however, for many niggling points remained to be settled, any one of which could have wrecked things. By the end of the year the Anglo-French agreement still hung in the balance, and it wasn't until May 1904 that the Entente was finally signed.

Into the future

THE EVENTS OF 1903 swept away decades of distrust. This in itself was fantastic enough but what it would mean for the future of Europe was still unclear. Germany, for one, was not worried, for she did not believe that the new friendship would last or that a formal agreement would ever be signed. Certainly few people anywhere foresaw that the Entente Cordiale would one day lead Britain into a major war at the side of France.

A real Anglo-French entente is in the long run impossible because in the colonial sphere differences will inevitably arise. Indeed, they will arise again very soon and these artificially spun threads will be severed with a jerk.
From the *Berlin Post*, 3 May

World News

US seizes Panama

IT HAD LONG BEEN an American ambition to shorten the long sea journey between her east and west coasts by cutting a canal through the Isthmus of Panama at the continent's narrowest point. When Colombia, whose territory it was, refused to co-operate, American agents stirred up a rebellion there. The Panama area then declared its independence and handed over some of its land to the USA as a canal zone. President Roosevelt had no doubts that such behaviour could be fully justified. Work on the canal began at once. It was completed in 1914.

The people of the US and the people of the Isthmus and the rest of mankind will all be better because we dug the Panama Canal and keep order in the neighbourhood. And the population and revolutionaries at Bogota are entitled to precisely the amount of sympathy that we extend to other bandits.
President Roosevelt to Congress, 8 December

German Socialists make big gains

THE GERMAN SOCIAL DEMOCRATIC PARTY (SPD) made big gains in the elections for the German Parliament or Reichstag, raising their number of seats from 56 to 81. This sent a shudder of fear through Germany's middle classes but had little effect on how the country was run, for the Reichstag held little real power.

Scandal in the Congo

UNLIKE OTHER COLONIES, the Congo in Central Africa belonged not to the Belgian nation but to King Leopold II himself. For over 20 years he had exploited the land and its people and pocketed the profits. In 1903 the British consul in Leopoldville, Sir Roger Casement, took a journey through the major rubber-producing areas. He published what he found there in a report that became known as the 'Black Diaries', which shocked even a Europe used to regarding the coloured peoples of the world as inferior.

It used to take ten days to get the twenty baskets of rubber – we were always in the forest, and then when we were late we were killed. We had to go further and further into the forest to find the rubber vines . . . and our women had to give up cultivating the fields and gardens. Then we starved . . . we begged the white men to leave us alone, saying we could get no more rubber, but the white men and their soldiers said: 'Go! You are only beasts yourselves'.
The testimony of a Congolese rubber-worker, from Sir Roger Casement's report to the British Foreign Office, 1903

A British view of Leopold's Congo.

IN THE RUBBER COILS.

Russian Marxists split

A LITTLE-NOTICED EVENT took place in London when members of the Russian Social and Democratic Labour Party held a conference there. As always, delegates quarrelled bitterly over tactics and principles. One section, under Vladimir Ulyanov or Lenin, advocated the restriction of party membership to a small band of professionals who would dedicate their lives to the revolution. Their opponents, under Martov and Plekhanov, argued for a more broadly-based party membership. Lenin's group won the day and were nicknamed Bolsheviks or 'Majority Men'. The minority group became known as Mensheviks. No one realized then what momentous consequences this split would have for the future of Russia and the world.

Lib-Lab pact

THE LRC'S FORTUNES were rising. In 1903 they won by-elections at Woolwich and Barnard's Castle. Now there was a danger that at the next election the anti-Conservative vote would be split, allowing the Tories to win again. Herbert Gladstone, the Liberal Chief Whip, and Ramsay MacDonald agreed together that neither party would put up candidates in constituencies that the other had a good chance of winning. Outside the top leadership of the two parties, this Lib-Lab pact was kept a closely-guarded secret.

Chamberlain puts the case for preferential tariffs – a Punch *cartoon.*

Tariff reform crusade begins

SOME BRITONS were becoming concerned about her loss of economic pre-eminence, as her industrial rivals were undercutting prices and might one day drive British workers out of work. Cheap grain from the USA was also harming local farmers. In a dramatic speech in Birmingham in May Joseph Chamberlain suggested that free trade, which had been a hallowed British tradition since the mid-nineteenth century, ought to be abandoned in favour of a system of Imperial Preference, in which the white empire would act as one economic unit, trading freely between themselves but putting up tariff barriers against outside competition. Farmers, manufacturers, most of the press and the Conservative Party backed the idea as a long-term means of ensuring full employment. The middle and working classes were sceptical, for in the short term, it would mean higher food prices that would badly hit the poor. The Liberals scented that opposition to Chamberlain's schemes would be a vote-winner. Their speakers took to carrying two loaves of bread around in their pockets. On the platform, they waved at their audiences the 'little loaf of protection' and the 'big loaf of free trade'. Suddenly, the future of the Liberal Party looked much brighter.

Agriculture, the greatest of all trades and industries, has been practically destroyed . . . Sugar has gone, silk has gone, iron is threatened, wool is threatened, the turn of cotton will come. . . At the present moment these industries and the working men who depend on them are like sheep in the field.
From a speech by Chamberlain in Birmingham, in October

Women demand the vote

THE LADYLIKE SOCIETIES of Victorian England that had campaigned for female suffrage had been consistently ignored by the all-male Parliament. Now some women's frustration reached boiling point. In Manchester, Mrs Emmeline Pankhurst and her daughters, Christabel and Sylvia, set up the Women's Social and Political Union (WSPU), which vowed to use whatever methods were necessary to force their case on public attention. Soon they were nicknamed Suffragettes.

Sport and the Arts

New play by Shaw

BRITAIN'S MOST POPULAR DRAMATIST was George Bernard Shaw, whose style was very different from his continental counterparts. The most important thing about a play, he argued, was not its realism but its relevance to the needs of the time. His characters, therefore, were not realistic individuals but mouthpieces through which contemporary issues could be discussed, with the help of witty and lively dialogue. All his plays have long prefaces explaining what they are trying to achieve. In 1903 his latest play, *Man and Superman*, a comedy with serious overtones about the battle of the sexes, in which women are shown to have the upper hand, opened in London and was a great success. It reflected Shaw's view, advanced for his time, that women were every bit as capable and strong-willed as men and did not deserve their second-class status.

It is assumed that the woman must wait, motionless, until she is wooed. Nay, she often does wait motionless. That is how the spider waits for the fly. But the spider spins her web. And if the fly, like my hero, shews a strength that promises to extricate him, how swiftly does she abandon her pretence of passiveness, and openly flings coil after coil about him until he is secured for ever!
From the Preface to *Man and Superman*

Some novels of 1903

The Ambassadors, one of the last novels by the American, Henry James.

The Call of the Wild, by Jack London, the classic tale of one man's struggle against the elements in the Canadian North.

Typhoon, another sea story by Joseph Conrad.

Buddenbrooks, by the German, Thomas Mann. An epic about the decline of a German middle-class family.

First action film

THE WORLD'S FIRST proper action feature film was made in the United States. It broke new ground in several ways. Edwin Porter's *The Great Train Robbery* told the story of a robbery, chase and the bringing of the criminals to justice in America's Wild West and was the forerunner of the classic Hollywood Western about the struggle between 'goodies' and 'baddies', in which the good side always won. It was also the first film in which the camera moved from scene to scene in order to create a sense of drama and tension, which is the basis of most modern film technique. It was shot without sound in black and white and lasted 12 minutes.

The forerunner of the modern Western: a still from The Great Train Robbery.

New sporting tradition

A SPORTING 'first' of 1903 became a tradition that has lasted to the present day. From time to time in the past informal tours had taken place between cricketers from England and Australia. Now these were taken over by the Marylebone Cricket Club (MCC), based at Lords, and 'test' matches between teams of the best players from England and the Commonwealth became an annual event. Every winter the MCC team toured Australia, New Zealand or South Africa (other countries like the West Indies were added later) and every summer they played host to a visiting team. In the MCC's first tour in the winter of 1903-4 they beat Australia by three games to two.

Spectators die in road race

ON THE OPENING DAY of the Paris to Madrid motor race in May six people died, including four bystanders. One driver plunged his car into a level-crossing keeper's cottage. The race was stopped and France then banned all racing on ordinary roads unless special arrangements had been made to clear the road beforehand.

The motor age begins

ALTHOUGH MOTOR CARS were still the playthings of the rich, they were becoming an increasingly familiar sight on the roads of Western Europe and the USA and causing new problems. By 1903 there were about 8000 private cars in Britain and 13,000 in France. The Chief Constable of Surrey was so outraged by the behaviour of drivers out from London on day trips that he declared 'war on the automobile'.

Sir,

In the interest of public safety in London, I venture to write to you the following letter, as the circumstance I relate occurred just as I was passing the spot.

Today, just after one o'clock, a man on a bicycle turned into Hyde Park by the western entrance at Hyde Park Corner; no sooner had he turned on his proper side than a motor car coming at high speed swerved over completely to the wrong side of the road and ran into the bicycle, smashing it and throwing the rider to the ground with such force that he was rendered insensible and had to be carried to St George's Hospital with serious injuries.

The motor car, without stopping at all, made off at high speed and so could not be identified. . . .

Letter to *The Times*, 19 March

As the result of so many complaints, a speed limit of 20 mph (32 km/h) was introduced in Britain in 1903 and cars had to carry a number plate for easier identification. Drivers did not yet have to pass a test, though, before they took to the road. In the same year the first motor taxis appeared on the streets of London and were accused of frightening the horses. In the USA Henry Ford set up the Ford Motor Company and vowed to make Detroit the 'motor capital of the world'.

The motoring age begins: Kensington High Street in 1903.

Man takes to the air

ON 17 DECEMBER, at Kitty Hawk in South Carolina, Orville Wright took off in a petrol engine-powered wooden aeroplane designed by himself and his brother, Wilbur. He stayed in the air for 59 seconds. This was the first flying machine ever to stay in the air entirely by its own power. The age of modern aviation had begun. At the time Europeans all but ignored the breakthrough. The French wrote it off as 'le bluff americain'.

A new food

THE SEARCH TO FIND a cheap but palatable alternative to butter was successful in 1903 when a method was found of hardening vegetable oils. The new product was named margarine and sold for about a third of the price of real butter. It became a staple food of the urban poor and often made a poor diet even worse. It was not until many years later that extra vitamins were added to it to make it as nutritious as butter.

Safer electricity

THE NEWCASTLE-ON-TYNE Electricity Company installed the first generator to produce alternating instead of direct electrical current. Alternating current sends out power in short bursts, not in a steady stream and is therefore much safer. Most modern electricity systems all over the world work like this.

1904 War in the

Russia opts for war

THE RIVALRY BETWEEN RUSSIA AND JAPAN in the Far East reached a climax in the first month of 1904. The Japanese were still smarting under the insult of being forced to give up Port Arthur and were suspicious of Russian troop movements in Manchuria. On her part, Russia seemed almost to be provoking a showdown with her rival. Discontent was running high at home and Tsar Nicholas II and his ministers may have hoped that a short, victorious war would divert people's attention from these problems. No one doubted that a great power like Russia would lick little Japan.

Japan strikes

THE JAPANESE had other ideas. Convinced by the beginning of 1904 that war was inevitable, she decided to strike first, before Russia could bring up reinforcements. At this time their navies were evenly matched, while Japanese ground troops outnumbered the Russians by three to one. But if Russia should be given time to bring in ships and soldiers from the West, the balance of forces would swing decisively the other way. On 6 February, without warning, Japan struck.

First round to Japan

WITH THE ADVANTAGE OF SURPRISE, the first round went to Japan. On 8 February a small squadron appeared off the coast of Korea and ordered the two Russian gunboats there to leave. As they did so, the Japanese ships opened fire on them, sinking them both. At the same time, the main Japanese fleet under Admiral Togo attacked the Russian Pacific fleet at anchor in Port Arthur. He was helped by the fact that the Russian Admiral's wife was giving a party on board the flagship, which was lit up for the occasion. Before the confused Russians realized what had hit them, the enemy had fired their torpedoes and fled, leaving Russia's two best battleships crippled. Togo then threw a blockade around the port, bottling up the Pacific fleet for the rest of the war.

A new force to be reckoned with: a picture drawn for a French magazine of the Japanese attack on Port Arthur.

Far East

Battle for Korea

NOW ABLE TO LAND TROOPS UNOPPOSED, the Japanese overran Korea. Outnumbered and incompetently led, the Russians retreated in disorder. On 1 May they made a stand on the Yalu River, which forms the border between Korea and Manchuria. The result was a decisive victory for the Japanese, the first time in modern history that a European army had been beaten by an Asiatic one.

It is no disrespect to the Japanese to confess that a lingering doubt remained in the mind of many soldiers, all the world over, upon the question of whether the troops of the Mikado would be able to stand up to the Russian enemy when it came to the push. That doubt has now been set at rest. . . The echoes of the battle will reverberate far, and distant is the day when the story of how a great empire was humiliated by a despised Oriental enemy will weary in the telling, especially among the races of the unforgiving East.

From an article in *The Times*, 3 May

Baltic fleet sets out

IN SEPTEMBER Russia's Baltic fleet set out for the Far East. It included five new battleships and was commanded by Admiral Rozhestvesky. Russian propaganda boasted that it would turn the course of the war around, but others were more sceptical. The voyage half way round the world would take eight months and give the Japanese plenty of time to get ready.

A lost opportunity

ON 15 MAY the war might have swung the other way when the Japanese fleet besieging Port Arthur ran into one of its own minefields. In full view of the Russians one Japanese battleship sank and another had to be towed away. But instead of exploiting the chaos that followed the Russians stayed quietly in harbour. A golden opportunity to turn the war around had been thrown away.

Port Arthur under siege

In the summer Japanese troops came up behind Port Arthur on the landward side and for six months, the Russians, helped by a well-planned system of trenches, defended stubbornly. The Japanese were made to pay heavily for every inch of ground they gained. At the same time over 100,000 fresh Russian troops poured into Manchuria from Europe, although many of them were undertrained and unenthusiastic reservists. The war looked as if it was going to deteriorate into stalemate.

10 October
Our own and the Japanese trenches are now so close that frequent and continuous rifle fire is inevitable, in which each side tries to spot the enemy and put a bullet into him. Our soldiers resort to the following method: one man fixes to his back a stick with a fur cap on the end and a greatcoat thrown over it and then crawls along the trench; the Japanese immediately open fire on the moving target, thus revealing themselves and making it possible to shoot one or other of their riflemen. . .
Meanwhile every day the burden of the siege becomes more and more noticeable. The cold is coming and at nights in the trenches it is almost freezing. In the light dugouts it is becoming uncomfortable, and in the trenches quite impossible. The danger from enemy shells and bullets grows all the time. Food is getting scarcer; for a long time there has been no meat, and tinned food is very short and we are treated to it rarely. Horsemeat is issued but cannot be increased because the horses are necessary for transporting shells and food to the positions. But our soldiers don't seem to notice all this and seem to be becoming even more cheerful and lively.
From the diary of a Russian sapper, who was killed during the siege.

Port Arthur falls

IN DECEMBER the Japanese captured 203 Meter Hill overlooking the port. From there they could lob shells directly into the town. Within three weeks the Pacific fleet had been destroyed, not from the sea but from the land. By the end of the year, Port Arthur was on the verge of surrender. The first year of the war had ended in disaster for Russia.

World News

Roosevelt re-elected

THEODORE ROOSEVELT had been a memorable President. As well as his dramatic action over the Panama Canal, he had taken up the cause of 'trust-busting' at home, where groups of companies merged into vast, price-fixing monopolies or trusts and drove smaller firms out of business. Aware that America was in danger of squandering her natural resources by allowing unchecked private development, many areas rich in minerals were taken out of private hands and put in Federal ownership. The first national parks were also set up. In November Roosevelt was re-elected as President with a large majority.

BRITISH SHIPS FIRED ON BY RUSSIAN FLEET.

EXTRAORDINARY OUTRAGE IN THE NORTH SEA.

HULL FISHING STEAMERS RAKED BY THE BALTIC FLEET WITH SHOT AND SHELL WITHOUT WARNING.

One Trawler Sunk, another Missing, and others Damaged with Loss of Life—Many Wounded—Amazing Action apparently Due to Fear of Attack by Japanese —Riddled Fleet Returns to Hull with its Dead—Statements by Eye-witnesses of the Attack — Baltic Fleet now in British Waters.

KILLED.	WOUNDED.
Capt. Geo. H. Smith	About 30 men
John Leggett	

US intervenes in Dominican Republic

WHEN THE TINY DOMINICAN REPUBLIC defaulted on her loans in January, the United States took over her finances and imposed a debt-paying schedule. Roosevelt argued a 'civilized' nation like the US had the right to 'police' the rest of the American continent and uphold law and order. This set the tone of US relations with her southern neighbours for the rest of the century.

Dogger Bank incident

IN OCTOBER the Russian Baltic fleet on route to the Far East ran into trouble in a bizarre way, while it was still thousands of miles from its goal. At dawn on 22 October, as the fleet passed over Dogger Bank in the North Sea, unidentified boats and flashes were seen on the horizon. They were vessels of the Hull fishing fleet signalling to each other with rockets, as was their custom. In panic, thinking they were Japanese torpedo boats waiting to ambush them, the Russians opened fire, sinking one vessel and damaging several others. Two English seamen were killed and a number wounded. In Britain there was an outcry and the popular press called for war. This the British government did not really want, and in the end she accepted an apology and a promise of compensation. The Baltic fleet sailed on. At the year's close she had reached the East African island of Madagascar.

Indignation in Britain over the Dogger Bank incident. The headline from the Daily Express *on 23 October.*

Revolt in South-West Africa

SERIOUS TROUBLE broke out in the German colony of South-West Africa. Since its seizure in the 1880s, the settlers and businessmen who had gone out there to make their fortunes had plundered the country's resources and exploited its inhabitants. Now the Herero tribe rose in rebellion, massacring German settlers. General von Trotha, who was sent out with a force of 15,000, saw this as a good opportunity to exterminate the Hereros as a race and confiscate their lands. The revolt was finally put down in 1906 at a cost of between 60,000 and 80,000 African lives.

The Hereros must leave the land. If they refuse I shall compel them with the gun. I shall assume charge of no more women and children, but shall drive them back to their people or let them be shot at.
General von Trotha, 1904

Fisher becomes First Sea Lord

ON 21 OCTOBER (Trafalgar Day) Admiral John Fisher was appointed First Sea Lord. He considered the British Navy as her lifeline in peace and in war, and believed it had been allowed to become dangerously antiquated. A modernization programme was immediately put underway. Obsolete ships were

Chinese labour scandal

AFTER THE BOER WAR there was a shortage of labour in the South African gold mines. The British government decided to import labourers from China, who would sign on to work for three years at much lower wages than white miners would accept. The first shipment arrived in May 1904 and by the end of the year there were 30,000 there. They were housed in compounds which they were not allowed to leave even in their off-duty hours. Many people in Britain regarded this system of indentured labour as little better than slavery. It made the Conservative government even more unpopular

Bloodshed in Tibet

IN DECEMBER 1903 the British force under Colonel Younghusband had invaded Tibet. On 13 January he was met by a representative from the Dalai Lama, who denied that there had ever been any Russians in Tibet at all. The Tibetans, Younghusband was told, wanted to be left alone. The British advance continued. At the end of March they met a Tibetan army, which surrendered without a shot being fired, until the British tried to disarm them. Now the Tibetans resisted, for they used their guns for hunting and faced starvation without them, but against Maxim guns they stood no chance and 700 were killed. There were no British dead. Many of the British soldiers, including Younghusband himself, were ashamed of what they had done. On 2 August the expedition reached Lhasa. There was more fighting and a further 200 Tibetans were killed. This time the British lost 40 men. But there were no Russians there, nor any sign that there ever had been: the Tibetans had been telling the truth. British high-handedness and the bloodshed to which it had led, which no one had really wanted, made her the object of much criticism abroad. Younghusband himself was virtually disowned by the embarrassed government, although he was guilty of nothing more than trying to carry out impossible orders. Altogether, it was one of the least creditable episodes in British Imperial history.

It was a loathsome sight, and however much I felt even then that it would probably work out well in the end, I could not but be disgusted at the sight of those poor wretched peasants mowed down by our rifles and Maxims.
From the diary of Colonel Younghusband, 30 March

British troops enter Lhasa, August 1904. Although the artist here makes it look like a triumph, there was little for Britain to be proud of in this one-sided contest.

scrapped and others converted from coal to oil. The first submarines were built and new training programmes for sailors were begun. The biggest change of all was the commissioning of a new super-battleship, HMS *Dreadnought*.

If the Navy is not supreme, no Army, however large, is of the slightest use. It's not invasion we have to fear if our Navy is beaten IT'S STARVATION.
From a memorandum written by Admiral Fisher, 28 July

Sport and the Arts

A new newspaper

ALFRED HARMSWORTH launched the *Daily Mirror*, the first newspaper to use a new technique of reproducing half-tone photographs and to devote as much space to pictures as to print. By the end of the decade it was selling a million copies a day, more even than the *Daily Mail*.

Short and sweet

FOR WOMEN WHO COULD AFFORD IT, fashions were still very elaborate, with wide, decorated hats and puffed sleeves being particularly popular. By 1904, however, there were signs that female dress was becoming more practical, even among the leisured classes. This year's skirts were slightly shorter than usual and a coat and skirt combination replaced the ordinary dress for daytime wear and out of doors.

Time was, not very long ago,
When Mabel's walking skirt
Trailed half-a-yard behind to show
How well she swept the dirt.
But 'short and sweet' are in again:
No more the grievance rankles,
For Mabel's now curtailed her train
And shows her dainty ankles.
Punch, 13 October

Some new productions of 1904
Madame Butterfly, a new opera by Puccini was performed at La Scala in Milan. It was unpopular at first but later became one of his most famous works.

Peter Pan or The Boy Who Never Grew Up by J.M. Barrie, a children's play that became a classic, was first performed at the Duke of York's Theatre in London on 28 December.

The Cherry Orchard, Chekhov's last play was performed in Moscow. He died later in the year.

What the well-dressed woman was wearing in the spring of 1904. At the same time, female clothing was becoming less fussy and restricting.

New educational opportunities

BECAUSE OF THE LACK of free higher education in Britain many working-class people were keen to make up the education they had missed. In 1904 a group of sympathetic university lecturers and trade union officials founded the Workers' Educational Association (WEA), whose aim was to provide low-cost, university-level courses at evening classes. The first WEA branches were in Reading, Derby, Rochdale and Ilford, offering courses in economics, economic history and literature. By 1914 the number of branches had risen to 179, with over 11,430 members, and the variety of courses offered had greatly increased.

Education should be a free and open highway upon which the only tolls are to be mental equipment and high character.
Albert Mansbridge, founder of the WEA

Sporting news

THE THIRD MODERN Olympic Games were held in conjunction with the St Louis World Fair in the USA. More people competed this time but most of them were Americans, who won nearly all the events. The only gold medallist not from the USA was Etienne Desmorteau of Canada, who won the shot-put. New sports introduced for the first time were boxing, lawn tennis and archery . The sensation of the Games was caused by Fred Lorz in the marathon. He accepted a lift in a lorry over part of the route, came in first and was denounced as he stood on the rostrum to receive his medal.

Even in this age of growing professionalism, the British amateur tradition remained strong. In a charity football match, the famous amateur side, Corinthian Casuals, took on Bury, who had won that year's FA Cup without conceding a goal. The Corinthians won 10-3!

A weapon of the future?

THE ROYAL NAVY took delivery of her first five submarines. Built in Barrow-in-Furness to an American design, each submarine was armed with one torpedo and powered by a petrol engine. Many old-fashioned sailors were sceptical about their value, but their supporters, including Sea Lord Fisher, saw them as the naval weapon of the future.

New motor firm founded

NEW COMPANIES making and selling motor cars mushroomed in these years. One of them began when an aristocratic car salesman, the Hon. Charles Stewart Rolls, teamed up with a Manchester electrical engineer, Henry Royce. They named their new firm Rolls-Royce. It went on to become one of the most famous names in the motoring world.

New York Subway opened

THE REVOLUTION in urban transport continued with the opening of the first line of the New York Subway. It was fully-electrified and ran for nine miles under the main thoroughfare of Broadway. Eventually it was to become the longest underground railway in the world.

Some 'firsts' of 1904

THE FRENCH FIRM of Michelin produced the first car tyre with a ridged, flat tread, of the type used today. It gave a much better grip on the road than the old smooth, rounded one had done.

The first gas-fired central-heating system was used to heat a school in Clapham, in South London.

This year also saw the first vacuum flask, for keeping liquids hot or cold, as well as the first coin-operated ticket machine on the London Underground.

Pavlov and his dogs

A RUSSIAN SCIENTIST, Ivan Pavlov, received the Nobel Prize for his work on conditioned reflexes in dogs. In his experiments, he had shown how once a dog had learned to associate food with the ringing of a bell, it would automatically salivate every time it heard that sound, even if there was no food around. Pavlov argued that this discovery might also help in understanding human behaviour. In time, his work became one of the bases of modern behavioural psychology.

The father of modern behavioural psychology: the Russian scientist Ivan Pavlov.

1905 Revolution

A long-expected event

FOR SOME YEARS people inside and outside Russia had talked of the inevitability of revolution there. Russia's extremes of wealth and poverty, her autocratic political system, which gave her people no say in the running of their country and her mixture of races and nationalities all provided fuel for the blaze to come. The humiliations of 1904 set it alight.

A bloody Sunday

ON 22 JANUARY the first clash took place. 200,000 striking workers from the factories of St Petersburg, the capital, accompanied by their wives and children and carrying no weapons but religious icons, gathered in front of the Tsar's Winter Palace to present a petition outlining their grievances. They were led by a mysterious priest, Father Gapon. The petition asked for improvements in living and working conditions and for political and civil rights. Most of the marchers were simple, illiterate men, who believed that the Tsar had been kept in ignorance of his people's suffering by his advisors. Once he knew the truth, all would be put right. They were wrong. The Tsar and his family had already fled to a place of safety, and the troops guarding the Palace opened fire on the petitioners. Within minutes, hundreds lay dead and over 3000 wounded, many of them women and children trampled to death in the ensuing panic.

We, working men and inhabitants of St Petersburg, our wives and our children and our helpless old parents, come to You, Sire, to seek for truth, justice and protection. We have been made beggars; we are oppressed; we are near to death.
From the petition of the workers of St Petersburg to the Tsar, 22 January

Men, women and children fell at each volley. The people, seeing the dead and dying carried away in all directions, the snow on the streets and pavements soaked with blood, cried aloud for vengeance. As the troops fired recklessly right and left, with or without reason, the people appealed to them, saying, 'you are Russians! Why play the part of bloodthirsty butchers?'
An eye-witness account, published in *The Weekly Times*, 27 January

Bloody Sunday: the scene outside the Winter Palace in St Petersburg, 22 January.

in Russia

Revolution sweeps the countryside. A French artist's impression of Russian peasants ransacking a wealthy home during 1905.

Disorder spreads

THIS WAS THE SIGNAL for an explosion of public feeling. As the news spread, strikes broke out in other large cities and in the universities. Peasants, the bulk of the Russian population, began plundering and burning the property of their landlords. And in the midst of the turmoil, news of the sinking of the Russian navy at the Battle of Tsushima came through.

Mutiny!

MUTINY IN THE ARMED FORCES followed. Sailors on the *Potemkin*, a battleship of the Black Sea fleet, began by protesting about rations and ended by murdering their officers and taking over their ship. For two months the *Potemkin* went on a rampage around the Black Sea gaining legendary status. Flying the Red Flag from her mast, she called on the coastal towns, inciting mutiny and strikes. The city of Odessa was shelled. When she ran out of fuel, she was taken to a Rumanian port, where the crew asked for asylum.

In the capital strikers set up a council of elected representatives from the shopfloor to co-ordinate strike action and formulate their demands. It was called the Soviet of Workers' Deputies. Trotsky was its first chairman.

The turning point

IN THE END Tsar Nicholas had to give in, although he did it reluctantly.

There were two ways open: to find an energetic soldier and crush the rebellion by brute force. But that would have meant rivers of blood, and we should only have been back where we started.
The other way out would be to give the people their civil rights. . . This would mean, of course, a constitution.
We discussed it for days and finally, invoking God's help, I signed. . . There was no other way.
From the diary of Tsar Nicholas II

In a manifesto issued on 30 October the Tsar promised civil liberties and a Duma, or Parliament, that would turn Russia into a constitutional monarchy like Britain. Most Russians accepted it with joy and went back to work. A great victory, it seemed, had been won.

The future

NOT EVERYONE was so optimistic. Revolutionaries like Trotsky warned that the October Manifesto was only a ruse to buy breathing space for the Tsar. What he had conceded in panic in 1905, he could just as easily take away again once the situation had calmed down. This was not The Revolution but merely a 'dress rehearsal'.

Do not hasten to celebrate victory: it is not yet complete. Does the promissory note weigh as much as pure gold? Is a promise of freedom the same as freedom?. . . The Tsar's manifesto, see! It is only a scrap of paper. Today it has been given us and tomorrow it will be taken away and torn into pieces as I am now tearing it into pieces, this paper-liberty, before your very eyes.
From a speech by Trotsky, 17 October

1905   World News

Russia humiliated

THE WAR IN THE FAR EAST continued to go badly for Russia. In March a week-long battle outside the town of Mukden in Manchuria ended in defeat and the surrender of nearly 156,000 Russian soldiers. The final humiliation came in May when the Baltic fleet was sunk in the Straits of Tsushima at the end of its eight-month journey. Both sides now wanted peace – Japan because she was in a strong bargaining position, Russia because she was faced with revolution at home. President Roosevelt offered to mediate.

President Theodore 'Teddy' Roosevelt.

A romantic view of colonialism in Morocco from a French postcard of the time.

Peace in the Far East

THE PEACE TREATY was signed at Portsmouth, New Hampshire, in September and was kinder to the Russians than they had expected, for the USA did not want to see an over-powerful Japan in the Pacific. Japan's predominence in Korea was recognized and Russia gave up Port Arthur, Manchuria and Sakhalin Island, but the large indemnity Japan demanded was not granted. The Japanese negotiators returned home to a stormy reception from a public who had expected more. Nevertheless, the crushing defeat of a European power by an Asiatic one had been a great shock and triggered off a frantic round of naval modernization everywhere.

Crisis over Morocco

MEANWHILE, an international crisis in Europe had brought France and Germany to the brink of war. The Entente Cordiale had given France a free hand in Morocco, in which the Germans had never shown any interest. On 5 March, however, the Kaiser landed in Tangier from his yacht, the *Hohenzollern*, and made a rousing speech to the small German community there, promising to do all he could to protect their interests. A month later he went a stage further and demanded an international conference to discuss Moroccan affairs. When the French Foreign Minister Delcassé refused, German threats of war frightened the French government so much that he was pressurized into resigning – a great humiliation for France. President Roosevelt intervened to calm passions down and set up a conference to meet in 1906 – the first time ever that the USA had intervened in a purely European quarrel.

A new nation

A NEW NATION came into existence when Norway gained independence from Sweden, who had ruled it since 1814. In a plebiscite the Norwegian people voted for a monarchy and chose a Danish prince as their new king. He took the name Haakon VII. His wife, Queen Maud, was the youngest daughter of Edward VII.

Revolt in East Africa

ANOTHER EXPLOITED German colony, Tanganyika, rose in revolt. The rebellious tribesmen called themselves Maji-Maji after the Swahili word for water, for they had been told by witch-doctors that the bullets of the white men would turn harmlessly to water; but before the rebellion was over, 70,000 Africans were dead.

Suffragettes go to prison

CHRISTOBEL PANKHURST and Annie Kenny were arrested in October after causing a disturbance at a meeting in Manchester during which they demanded that the speaker, Liberal MP Sir Edward Grey, publicly commit himself to their cause. On refusing to pay their fine, they were both sent to prison for seven days.

Come march with us to victory; come join the battle song
Of women chained to labour, who are suffering grievous wrong.
In a free land we are free not; minds equal have no place.
Men treat as merest playthings the mothers of the race.
We teach the little sons of men; we help the direst poor;
We nurse the wounded soldier, and fight the

Unrest in India

LORD CURZON, Viceroy of India, announced a scheme to partition the large province of Bengal in order to make it easier to administer. To his surprise, this caused outrage among educated Indians, as it had been made without any attempt at consulting Indian opinion. A campaign of violence against British rule began, and the incoming Viceroy, Lord Minto had several bombs thrown at him. No longer was Britain's right to rule over the sub-continent of 300 million people accepted without question.

Government resigns

IN DECEMBER Balfour's government resigned. His motives were devious, for an election would have to be held in 1907 anyway, and if it were fought by the Liberals as the Opposition, they would have the great advantage of being able to blame the Conservatives for all the country's troubles. If, however, the Liberals had to spend time in office first, their internal squabbles might pull them apart and give the Conservatives the electoral edge. Much to everyone's surprise, Liberal leader Campbell-Bannerman managed to put together a cabinet out of men who only a few years before had quarrelled bitterly over the Boer War. Asquith was Chancellor of the Exchequer, Sir Edward Grey Foreign Secretary and the young radical David Lloyd George was President of the Board of Trade. Winston Churchill, who had defected from the Conservatives in 1904, was appointed as Under-Secretary for the Colonies.

evil doer;
Yet in the council of the state, we have no voice or say
No voice in making cruel laws we may not disobey.
Suffragette marching song, 1905

Sport and the Arts

Art shock!

AN EXHIBITION held in Paris during the autumn by a group of painters calling themselves 'Les Fauves' or 'The Wild Beasts' caused a commotion. Their aim, they explained, was not to paint objects or scenes as they appeared superficially to the eye, but to use shape, colour and perspective to capture something of the 'inner reality' of things. Instead of natural shades, for example they painted in vivid primary colours. Leading painters of this school were Henri Matisse and André Derain.

Some outstanding paintings at the Paris exhibition

Matisse's portrait of his wife, with a green stripe across her forehead and down her nose.

Derain's portrait of Matisse, in which the face is half turquoise and the beard made up of daubs of brilliant crimson and black.

The landscapes of Maurice de Vlaminck, in which trees were often bright pink and skies green.

First cinema opened

THE WORLD'S FIRST purpose-built cinema opened in a converted warehouse in Pittsburgh in America. It contained 92 seats, a piano to provide background music and ran a continuous show from 8 am until midnight. The first film put on was *The Great Train Robbery*. As seats cost 5 cents, or a nickel, it was nicknamed the Nickelodeon.

Two new operas

TWO OPERAS first performed in 1905 created something of a stir, although in different ways. Franz Lehar's light-hearted operetta, *The Merry Widow*, which opened in Vienna became one of the most popular light operas of all time. When it came to London in 1907, it ran for two years without a break. Richard Strauss' *Salome*, on the other hand, with its overpowering, emotional music and its erotic dance of the seven veils, delighted some and scandalized others. After watching it, the Kaiser, who had recently appointed Strauss as Director of the Royal Opera, was heard to mutter, 'That's a nice snake I've reared in my bosom'.

Soccer's popularity spreads

THE POPULARITY of professional football was spreading to the South of England. Three new London teams, Chelsea, Charlton Athletic and Crystal Palace, were formed in 1905 and admitted to Division II, which was expanded to include 20 clubs. This year also saw the first four-figure transfer fee when Middlesborough payed Sunderland £1000 for Alf Common. Pessimists predicted that the time was coming when a few wealthy clubs, who could afford to buy up all the best players, would dominate the football scene, driving out smaller clubs and killing off amateurism.

Some new books of 1905

Where Angels Fear to Tread, the first novel by E.M. Forster, who was to write *A Passage to India* in the 1920s.

Professor Unrat, by the German author, Heinrich Mann. This was made into a famous film, *The Blue Angel* in the 1920s.

The Scarlet Pimpernel, by Baroness Orczy, a classic adventure story set during the French Revolution.

A Modern Utopia, by the English writer H.G. Wells, which was a fantasy about an ideal society of the future, in which the advances of modern technology are used for the benefit of all. This book had a serious social purpose. Wells also published *Kipps*, a novel about the fortunes of an ordinary man in the same year.

A new cricket star

JACK HOBBS, playing in his first season for Surrey, attracted attention with his natural batting talent. He scored 88 runs in the second innings of his first game and 155 in the next. He went on to become one of England's most famous cricketers. Yorkshire won the County Championship this year, for the fourth time in six years.

A new dimension

A YOUNG GERMAN MATHEMATICIAN, Albert Einstein, turned man's understanding of how the universe worked upside down, when he published his Special Theory of Relativity. There were, he argued, no absolute values like weight or time. Everything was relative to the speed at which the observer was travelling and had no relevance outside the earth's gravity. The amount of energy given off by an object also depended on its speed or velocity and could be expressed by the equation $E=MC^2$, where C equals the speed of light and M equals its mass. These ideas are difficult for the ordinary person to grasp, but have become the basis of all modern physics, including nuclear physics.

Albert Einstein, the father of modern physics.

Railways electrified

IN MANY BIG CITIES urban railway systems were being changed over from steam power to electric. The conversion of the London Underground was completed in 1905. Now that engines no longer gave off smoke, smaller rounder tunnels were built, which gave London's subway the popular nickname 'the tube'. Above ground, the Long Island Railroad in the USA, which took commuters into New York from the suburbs, became the world's first completely electrified suburban railway system. At the same time London's horse-drawn and steam trams were replaced by electric ones that ran on rails down the middle of the street. Tramways were to become a prominant feature of most European towns by 1914. It meant cleaner and more comfortable travel, but, as usual, not everyone thought the change was for the better.

The new all-electric underground: National Graphic *magazine's feature on the opening of a new line.*

'Twas not sweet of old, as our love we told
On the top of the old steam car,
When a wand'ring breeze made us cough and sneeze,
With a smell like rotten eggs and tar!

But the lights were low, and the pace was slow,
And the corner seats were cozy,
And many a Miss has received a kiss
On top of the car
From Perry Bar
Or the tram that came from Moseley!
From a postcard sold in Birmingham, 1905

Some 'firsts' of 1905

The first illuminated track diagram was installed in a London signal box. Train movements were indicated by small electric lights on a map, and the signalman no longer had to rely on his view of the line. The system has changed little since then.

The Pathé Company of France invented a technique for the rapid colouring of movie film, which had previously had to be done by hand, frame by frame. Now colour feature films were possible, although the new technique was not widely used until much later.

Shatter-proof glass, which was made by placing a sheet of celluloid between two panes of glass. This was a great boost to the modern 'glass and steel' school of architecture.

Rayon, an artificial silk, was manufactured by Courtauld's of Britain. Much cheaper than real silk and easier to care for than cotton, it was to become the most popular dress fabric by 1914.

An operation to insert an artificial hip joint, which increased mobility and provided relief from the pain of arthritis.

1906 San Francisco

A booming city

AT THE BEGINNING of 1906 San Francisco was a booming city of 350,000 people and was the chief port and commercial centre on America's thriving West coast. Her main streets were lit by electric light and her urban transport system of electrified cable cars was among the most advanced in the world.

San Francisco ravaged by the earthquake.

City swept by fire

WITHIN MINUTES fires broke out all over the city, as lamps and stoves overturned. Nearly all the water mains had been fractured in the earthquake and the fire brigade was helpless. A strong wind blowing off the bay fanned the flames. By 8 am the fire was beyond control and looked set to destroy those buildings that had escaped the worst effects of the quake.

Eye witness accounts

AN AWFUL CALAMITY has befallen San Francisco, which in magnitude makes the recent Vesuvius eruption trivial. It was exactly 5.18 this morning that the city was tossed about as a feather by the wind. The earth seemed to sink a moment; then buildings rose in the air like balloons; then there was a sort of sinking whose like mortal never experienced; then the clustered buildings of the town rocked like poplars in a storm.
J.P. Barrett, *New York Journal,* evening edition 18 April

I awoke on Wednesday to hear the groaning of timbers, a grinding and a creaking sound, and then a roaring in the street. The plaster and wall decorations fell and it was as if the building was writhing. The darkness was intense. The air was rent by the screams of women. I jumped out of bed and crawled towards the door. The twisting and writhing appeared to increase. I wrenched open the door which swung back against my shoulder. Just then the building seemed to steady and right itself but I went outside, for I could not believe the building could endure such a shock and still stand. . .
Dr Flemming, a doctor from Los Angeles who was staying at the Palace Hotel, which survived the earthquake but not the fire. Reported in *The Times,* 21 April

9 AM, 18 April
The Palace Hotel is burning. The gas works south of Market Street have blown up and started another huge fire.
10.15 am
The flames are now nearing the offices of the telegraph company where I am sitting. If the building catches fire, San Francisco will be cut off from the outside world.
Reports reaching New York on the afternoon of 18 April, reported in *The Times,* 19 April

RUINS OF THE CITY AFTER EARTHQUAKE AND FIRE 1906 SAN FRANCISCO, CAL.

Earthquake hits San Francisco

AT 5.18 AM on the morning of the 18 April the city was struck by a devastating earthquake that was so strong it registered on seismographs as far away as Australia and Vienna. The main shock lasted about three minutes and was followed by a number of smaller tremors. In the city centre buildings collapsed into the street, burying hundreds alive in the rubble. Worst affected were the flimsy tenement buildings, where many of San Francisco's poorest citizens lived. These collapsed like card houses.

Destroyed

Population camps in the streets

IN FACT the fires raged for three days and completed the almost total destruction of the city. The telegraph office was an early victim and reporters had to cross the Bay to Oakland by boat to file their stories.

The homeless citizens camped out in the city's parks and squares, and for several days thousands of refugees were without food or drinking water. Martial law was declared.

9.15 19 April
San Francisco is practically destroyed. . .
You cannot send us too many tents; 200,000 or more people are homeless. Food is very scarce. The provision houses are all destroyed.
From General Funston, officer in command in San Francisco, to Washington.

A man has been shot. . . for being discovered by a patrol in the act of using precious drinking water for washing his hands and face.
Daily Mail, 23 April

After the earthquake: citizens walk among the ruins of their city.

Man begs to be shot

We watched soldiers and firemen trying to remove from a burning building, the front of which had fallen out, a man who was pleading piteously to be put out of his misery. His head and shoulders projected from the rubble, with his free hand he was trying to help the firemen by pulling at the timbers. One by one the men were driven back by the approaching flames until one only remained. He was blistered by the heat. . . A sheet of flame swept round the corner of the building; the soldier picked up his rifle and turned to go. From where we stood we could see a beam pinning the man down. His hair was smouldering and his moustache singed. 'For God's sake shoot me', he begged. . . . We heard the crack of the rifle and knew that he had done so.

An eye witness account by an Englishwoman, who was evacuated to Los Angeles on 20 April. Reported in *The Times* 21 April

The final toll

BY THE EVENING OF THE 23RD the worst fires had burnt themselves out, leaving the city a smouldering ruin. Only 500 had died but 250,000 – two-thirds of the city's population – were homeless. 28,000 buildings, covering 49 sq.m. (127 sq.km.) had been destroyed. Many insurance companies, that had to pay up for the estimated $400 million in damages, faced bankruptcy. Few people had any hesitation in classifying this as the worst disaster in American history.

City to be rebuilt

IN SPITE OF WARNINGS by scientists that San Francisco was built astride a geological fault – the San Andreas Fault – and that another devastating earthquake was only too likely in the future, the citizens were determined to rebuild the city in the same place. They were heartened by evidence that modern buildings with steel frames had withstood the actual shock, even those that were twenty storeys high. It was the old-fashioned timber-frame structures that had collapsed. On 23 April the New York correspondent of the London *Times* took the train from Chicago to the West Coast. It was full of native San Franciscans, who had been away when the earthquake struck, who were going home to start rebuilding. The journalist had no doubt that they meant what they said.

The sons and grandsons of the 'Forty-niners' have inherited their forefathers' spirit and enterprise. They mean to rebuild San Francisco and declare that a new and more beautiful city will be complete in five years.
The Times, 24 April

World News

Germans rebuffed

THE INTERNATIONAL CONFERENCE on Morocco met at Algeciras in January and went on until April. The Germans had a good case, but the aggressive tone in which they defended their rights offended the British and fuelled the growing suspicion that Germany was a threat to world peace. They backed the French. The outward result was a draw. France was granted control of the Moroccan police, to be shared with Spain, while Germany obtained acceptance of her view that the problem of Morocco concerned all the powers. But the most important results had already taken place behind the scenes, for Britain and France had drawn closer together. A party of senior British officers had even gone to Paris to discuss how the two nations could work together in the hypothetical event of a joint war against Germany. Germany's hope that the Entente Cordiale would soon shatter were proving vain.

Asia on the move

THE RUSSO-JAPANESE WAR gave new confidence to Asian peoples, who throughout the nineteenth century had been forced to bow before superior European armed might. The first decade of the twentieth century saw the stirring of nationalist movements in India, Persia, China and Egypt, which did not look backwards to the past, as the Boxers and the Hereros had done, but planned to use modern technology and ideas like socialism and liberalism to give them the strength and unity to fight for independence. It was in 1906 that shrewd European observers first noticed what was going on under the surface of Asian society.

It seems to me that a change must be coming over the East. The victory of Japan has . . . had a remarkable influence. . . Moreover, the Russian revolution has had a most astounding effect here. Events in Russia have been watched with great attention, and a new spirit would seem to have come over the people. . . Who knows? Perhaps the East is really awakening from its slumber, and we are about to witness the rising of these patient millions against the exploitation of an unscrupulous West.
From a letter to *The Times*, 19 May, by a Swedish explorer travelling in Persia (Iran)

Russia experiments with democracy

IN THE EARLY MONTHS of 1906 Russia's first-ever parliamentary elections took place. The result confirmed the Tsar's worst fears, for the Duma was swamped by men who saw the October Manifesto as only the first in a series of changes. They went straight into the attack, demanding sweeping social and political reforms. Outraged, the Tsar dissolved the Duma and called for new elections. Russia's first experiment with democracy had ended in uproar.

Justice at last

IN 1894 a French Jewish army officer, Alfred Dreyfus, had been found guilty of spying for Germany, court-martialled and sent to Devil's Island. Many Frenchmen suspected that Dreyfus had been framed, perhaps because of his religion, and the 'Dreyfus Affair' had bitterly divided the nation. Now, after a re-investigation, Dreyfus was pronounced officially innocent. A great injustice had been righted.

Liberals win a landslide victory

BALFOUR'S CRAFTY ATTEMPT to outmanoeuvre the Liberals failed, for Campbell-Bannerman called an immediate general election to be held in January 1906. The Liberals emphasized all the unpopular things the Conservatives had done over the past six years, like introducing the 1902 Education Act, tariff reform and the importation of Chinese labour, that had offended one group or another and won a crushing victory by 377 seats to 157. Aided by the Lib-Lab Pact, the Labour Party won a surprising 29 seats.

Many people saw the election result as a watershed in British politics. The gap between rich and poor was widening but the underprivileged were no longer content to suffer in silence. Liberals, Lloyd George warned his colleagues, would have to adapt or perish.

I have one word for Liberals. I can tell them what will make this Labour Party a great and sweeping force in this country – a force that will sweep away Liberalism amongst other things. If at the end of an average term of office it were found that a Liberal Parliament had done nothing to cope with the social condition of the people, to remove the degradation of slums and widespread poverty and destitution in a land glittering with wealth . . . then would a real cry arise in

State of the art technology: HMS Dreadnought.

this land for a new party, and many of us here in this room would join in that cry.
Lloyd George in a speech made at Cardiff in October

For their part, Conservatives saw this not as an ordinary election defeat but as a threat to the lifestyles and values of the rich.

What has occurred has nothing to do with any of the things we have been squabbling about over the last few years. Campbell-Bannerman is a mere cork, dancing on a torrent of the same movement which has produced massacres in St Petersburg, riots in Vienna and socialist processions in Berlin.
From a letter from Arthur Balfour to his aunt, written in January

Cautiously, the Liberals made two concessions to the new age in 1906. The Trades Disputes Act gave full legal and economic immunity to trade unions that went on strike, and local authorities were given permission to provide free school meals for needy children.

Dreadnought

THE FIRST DREADNOUGHT was launched in October. It had taken just a year and a day to build and had cost £1¾ million. It had ten 12in. guns (more than twice as many as carried by any previous warship) and ran on oil as well as coal. It made every other battleship in the world, including all the other British ones, obsolete, and was bound to trigger off a naval arms race.

Novel's revelations shock America

UPTON SINCLAIR'S *The Jungle* was one of the most influential American novels of its generation. It is the story of a newly-arrived immigrant from Lithuania, who takes a job in Chicago's stockyards, where cattle from all over the country are slaughtered and turned into meat products, and is almost destroyed by the poverty and brutality of his life there. Sinclair had intended the book to be a plea for socialism, as the only way for a just society. Rather than troubling Americans' consciences, however, it revolted their stomachs. The outcry did not lead to revolution but to the passing of a Pure Food and Drugs Act by the Roosevelt government.

The streets through which Jurgis and Ona walked . . . were full of great hollows full of stinking green water. In these pools the children played, and rolled about in the mud of the streets. . . One wondered about the swarms of flies which hung about the scene, literally blackening the air, and the strange fetid odour which assaulted one's nostrils, a ghastly odour, of all the dead things in the universe.
From *The Jungle* by Upton Sinclair

Women warned off 'rough' sports

ALTHOUGH LIFE FOR WOMEN was still very restricted, things were slowly changing and more opportunities were opening up to them. Not everyone approved. In March an American doctor, Dudley Sergant, spoke out against the growing fashion for playing sports like hockey, lacrosse, netball and basketball, which were, in his opinion, making women unfeminine and harming their health. They should stick to graceful and gentle pastimes like gymnastics and tennis, he said.

Entertainment for everyone

THE MOST POPULAR form of entertainment in England, which before long was to be superseded by the cinema, was the music hall. Set in sumptuous surroundings with low admission prices, the acts were a mixture of the bawdy and the sentimental, often mixed with political satire. The audience were encouraged to join in. Among the stars of the time were Marie Lloyd, whose songs were considered rather 'naughty', Vesta Tilley and George Robey.

Entente Cordiale
A French lady grabbed me when I got outside.
'Oh! Voulez-vous, s'il vous plait, treat me,' she cried.
I said: 'My young lady, we've not met before.
So why should I treat you to things I abhor'.
She replied: 'Get along, I'm yer cousin-in-law'.
Oh, isn't it singular!

Chorus:
Oh, isn't it singular,
Awfully, very peculiar,
That new cousin I found
Cost me over five pound,
Oh, isn't it singular!
Music hall song of 1906, a typical mixture of the political and the bawdy

First Grand Prix held

ON 26 AND 27 JUNE the first proper Grand Prix motor race was held on a purpose-built circuit at Le Mans in France. For the first time drivers could test their skills to the limit. The 768 mile (1236 km) race (12 laps of 64 miles (103 km) each) was won by a Hungarian, Ferenc Szisz, in a Renault car at an average speed of 62.8 mph (101 km/h).

A star of the age: Vesta Tilley in music hall costume.

Published

A MAN OF PROPERTY, by John Galsworthy, the first novel in the Forsyte Saga about a late-Victorian middle-class family and the struggle within it between money and status on the one hand, and love and artistic sensibilities on the other.

More people living in towns

THE NINETEENTH-CENTURY trend towards living in towns was still gathering pace and some of the world's largest cities were becoming sprawling conurbations. Modern living patterns were already becoming clear. The poor congregated in the old inner cities, which were already beginning to fall into decay, while all who could afford it – the skilled workers and the middle classes – moved out to the suburbs and commuted to work each day on the new, efficient urban transport systems. With the arrival of motor vehicles, sky-scrapers and electric wires, towns took on a look that is familiar today. They also began to experience the less pleasant sides of urban living like traffic congestion, road accidents and pollution by vehicle exhausts.

Population of cities (in millions)	
London	4.5
New York	4
Paris	2.7
Berlin	2
Tokyo	1.9
St Petersburg	1.4
Vienna	1.3

Shoppers in a London street. City living was becoming the way of life for more and more people.

Medical news

BELGIAN SCIENTISTS succeeded in isolating the whooping cough bacillus and cultivating it in the laboratory. This was an essential first step towards developing a vaccine against a disease that killed thousands of small children every year, although some people have since argued that the vaccine itself is as dangerous as the disease.

Voices through the air

AN AMERICAN, Lee de Forest, had just invented the triode valve, which was far more efficient at picking up faint radio signals and transmitting them than earlier types of valves had been. For the first time it became possible to broadcast the human voice, and not just morse code, over long distances. On Christmas Eve the first successful radio broadcast was made from a station in Massachusetts by Reginald Fessenden. The programme began with violins playing 'Silent Night', followed by verses from St Luke's Gospel and ending with a Christmas greeting. The broadcast could be heard over a radius of 100 miles (161 km)

World's longest railway tunnel opened

THE SIMPLON TUNNEL under the Alps, linking France and Italy, was opened in May. It was 12½ miles (20 km) long and cost £3 million to build. When the two gangs of men working from each end met in the middle, the two shafts were only 8in. (20.3 cm) apart and 3in. (7.6 cm) different in height. The Simplon Tunnel remained the world's longest railway tunnel until the Japanese Seikan Tunnel was opened in the 1980s.

Some 'firsts' of 1906

Air-conditioning system, installed in a printing works in New York.

Permanent wave technique, for curling hair, which was soon nicknamed a 'perm'.

Colourprint film for cameras.

1907 Armed Camps

New winds blowing in London and St Petersburg

IN THE YEARS AFTER 1904 some rethinking had been going on in London and St Petersburg. After her defeat by Japan, Russia no longer seemed to Britain the formidable enemy she had been before, whereas Germany's aggressive talk and her naval programme excited considerable suspicion. Both Britain and Russia were worried about German plans to build a railway from Constantinople to the Persian Gulf – the so-called 'Berlin to Baghdad line' – which they saw as a possible forerunner to German control over the Middle East. Suddenly the Anglo-Russian quarrels of the past seemed less important than the fears they now shared.

The dogs of war foiled by peace: Punch's *comment on the* Triple Entente. *Not everyone thought the result of the 1907 Convention would be as simple as this.*

Rumours!

THROUGHOUT THE EARLY MONTHS of 1907 roumours circulated in the two capitals that secret negotiations were going on to settle outstanding disputes between the two old rivals. All the rumours were strenuously denied by the governments concerned.

From an authorised source I learn that reports emanating from St Petersburg in reference to the imminent conclusion of an Anglo-Russian agreement are devoid of any foundation.
The Times correspondent in St Petersburg, 1 March

The entirely premature reports about Anglo-Russian negotiations in progress are believed in Paris to emanate from the Wilhelmstrasse in Berlin and to have been set in motion with a distinct object. That object is to create a current of opinion in Russia hostile to friendship with Britain.
The Times correspondent in Paris, 24 May

Agreement reached

IN FACT THE RUMOURS were true. Talks had been going on since the middle of 1906, and on 31 August an Anglo-Russian convention was signed, similar to the one signed with France three years earlier. It was not a treaty of alliance but a settlement of outstanding quarrels in Tibet, Afghanistan and Persia, which would end the likelihood of war breaking out over these areas. The new friendship between Britain, France and Russia was dubbed the Triple Entente.

Reaction in Britain

NOT EVERYONE in Britain was pleased. Some, like Lord Curzon, felt that British interests in the East, which had been jealously guarded for so long, had been casually thrown away and that the Russians could never really be trusted. Others, including some Liberals and most Labour MPs, felt uncomfortable at making friends with an autocratic regime that mistreated its own people.

Mr Cunningham-Grahame proposed a resolution protesting against the establishment of friendly relations with the Government at St Petersburg on the grounds that the Russian Government was at war with the Russian people and that the proposed agreement would give it Great Britain's moral and material support in its barbarous methods of suppressing popular rights. He contended that the British Government had placed itself on a par with the Russian tyrants.
Report of a public meeting held on 18 September to protest against the Entente with Russia, *The Times*, 19 September

in Europe

PUNCH, OR THE LONDON CHARIVARI.—September 11, 1907.

BAFFLED!

[The new Anglo-Russian agreement is considered to be another earnest of peace.]

Alarm and Delight in Europe

ON THE SURFACE, the Anglo-Russian Convention was a boost to world peace, for the two nations were not ganging up on anyone else, only trying to settle their own longstanding quarrels. Neither the French nor the Germans saw it that way, though. The French were jubilant and claimed Britain as a new ally against France's old rival, Germany. In Germany, where the convention was seen as a plot to encircle the country with a ring of enemies, there was outrage. Plans were drawn up immediately for an increase in the size of the German army and for more armaments to be produced. Three new battleships were ordered. Sections of the press took on an even more aggressive and warlike tone.

Yes! It now appears as though they want to encircle us. We will know how to bear that. The Germans have never fought better than when forced to defend themselves.
Berlin Post, 3 September

Arms Race Hots Up

AS GERMANY stepped up her military build-up, it was likely that her neighbours would follow suit and an arms race be added to the naval race. Some worried observers saw the Anglo-Russian Convention not as a boost to peace but as a further stage in the division of Europe into two armed camps. After this, every minor crisis would bring with it the danger of widespread war.

United against war

EVERY YEAR DELEGATES from the Socialist parties of Europe held a congress to co-ordinate their tactics and lay the groundwork for a truly international working-class movement. In 1907 they met in Stuttgart in South Germany. In the wake of the war scares of 1905-6, the main topic of debate was what the working class could do to stop war if it came. After days of debate it was agreed that an international general strike should be called, which would paralyse the railways and telegraph and make mobilization impossible. An even more daring suggestion by the Russian Bolshevik, Lenin, that the opportunity ought to be seized to rouse the people to class war and thereby hasten to overthrow the capitalist system was rejected. Confidence ran high in the power of organized labour to control the destiny of Europe.

Democracy fails in Russia

RUSSIA'S FIRST ATTEMPT at democracy was stifled early in 1907 by the new Prime Minister, Stolypin. The second Duma, which met in April, was just as obstreperous as the first and just as quickly dismissed. Before new elections were held, Stolypin cleverly manipulated the electoral law so that most influence now lay with the wealthy landowners, who had most to lose by reform. The result was a tame third Duma, willing to rubber-stamp the Tsar's wishes and offering little criticism. It lasted its full term until 1912.

A new face at the Russian court: the monk, Gregory Rasputin, whose sinister influence was to grow over the years and help bring down a dynasty.

Democracy spreads

ELSEWHERE, the trend towards democracy continued, in spite of strenuous opposition to it by most of Europe's crowned heads. After a general strike in Vienna, the conservative Austro-Hungarian Empire introduced universal male suffrage, although this did not mean much, as the parliament there had little real power. In Norway and Finland women over 21 were given the vote.

Sinister influence at Russian court

A LITTLE-NOTICED EVENT took place at the Russian court, which was to have momentous consequences in years to come. The Tsar and Tsarina, who were deeply religious, were introduced to a wandering holy man, Father Gregory Rasputin. From the start he had a remarkable, soothing influence on their small son, the Tsarevitch Alexis, who suffered from haemophilia. Tsarina Alexandra fell completely under his spell and his influence over the court began to grow.

The Conservatives strike back

IN BRITAIN, the Liberal majority in the Commons was unassailable, but in the House of Lords Liberal Peers were outnumbered ten to one by Conservative ones. It was through the Lords, therefore, that Balfour chose to hit back. With increasing regularity, Liberal legislation that had passed through the Commons with ease was thrown out by the Upper House. Liberals became frustrated and angry. Lloyd George nicknamed the Lords 'Mr Balfour's poodle' and talk of restricting the powers of the House of Lords or even abolishing it altogether became commonplace.

In order to give effect to the will of the people as expressed by their elected representatives, the power of that House to amend or reject bills passed by this House must be so restricted as to secure that within the life of a single Parliament the final decision of the Commons should prevail.
Resolution by Campbell-Bannerman in the Commons, 24 June

Most people still lived in poverty. A London slum.

Growing concern about the nation's children

THERE WAS GROWING CONCERN about the poor health of many of Britain's children. In 1907 a schools medical service was set up, which is still in operation today. Doctors and nurses had to visit every school in their area and keep a record of each child's health and medical progress. This way, it was hoped that some of the commoner deformities and deficiency diseases like rickets might be checked. A London doctor, Dr Sykes, set up the country's first infant welfare clinic in the St Pancras district, modelled on one he had seen at Ghent in Belgium which gave mothers advice on how to look after their babies. In Birmingham a poster campaign gave tips on infant feeding and how to take care of children in hot weather. Critics pointed out that such measures only tinkered with the problem, which would not be solved until poverty itself was eradicated. However, the infant mortality rate did begin to drop a bit.

New opportunities for children

AN EDUCATION ACT made it compulsory for local authorities in Britain to reserve a quarter of their grammar school places as free places for bright children from poor homes, who would otherwise have had to leave school at 12. Many benefited from this but as many were excluded, for there were no free uniforms or books. And critics argued that the curriculum of the new grammar schools was all wrong. It concentrated too much on Latin and Greek, rather than on science and technology, and did little to prepare Britons for the competitive world of the future.

Sport and the Arts

A new style of painting

TWO YOUNG ARTISTS, Pablo Picasso and Georges Braque, caused a sensation when they put on an exhibition of their work in Paris, which took the anti-realism revolution in art a stage further. Their aim was to express the basic geometry underlying natural objects and to present the same thing from several different angles in the same picture. Colours were kept deliberately muted in order not to distract from the all-important geometric patterns. This style of painting was called Cubism and was the forerunner of modern abstract art. The single picture that attracted most attention was Picasso's *Les Demoiselles d'Avignon* (The Young Ladies of Avignon).

Playboy causes a riot

WHEN THE IRISH PLAYWRIGHT J.M. Synge's *The Playboy of the Western World*, set in a remote village in Ireland, was put on at the Abbey Theatre in Dublin, the candour of some of its language caused a riot in the audience. Synge defended himself on the ground that he was only copying the vigour and richness of everyday peasant speech and that his drama was more realistic than Chekhov's had ever been. Synge's work was part of a general revival of Irish culture that took place at this time and contributed to a rebirth of Irish national pride.

A popular summer sport: May Sutton plays lawn tennis at Wimbledon.

British domination of Wimbledon broken

BRITISH TENNIS PLAYERS had dominated the Wimbledon championships since they began in 1877. In 1907, however, all three titles were won by foreigners. Norman Brooks of Australia won the men's singles, Miss May Sutton of the USA the ladies' singles and Brooks and Wilding of New Zealand the doubles. In that year the Prince of Wales became President of the club and gave it a trophy to be awarded to the winner of the men's event. It is the one still in use today.

British reading habits

ALTHOUGH LITERACY was more widespread than ever before, most people did not regard reading as an important part of their lives. The philanthropist Lady Bell carried out a survey of 200 working-class homes in Middlesborough to find out what people actually read and discovered, not surprisingly, that most people did not care for 'high-brow' literature.

Reading Habit in 200 Middlesborough homes
There are:
17 women who cannot read
8 men who cannot read
28 houses where no one cares to read
8 men who actually dislike reading
3 women who actually dislike reading
7 women who say they 'have no time for it'
50 houses where they only read novels
58 houses where they read the newspapers only
37 houses where they are 'fond of reading' or 'great readers'

25 houses where they read books that are absolutely worth reading (this includes men who read books about their work)
From '*At the works*' by Lady Florence Bell

The best-selling novel of 1907 was by an author who has since been all but forgotten. *Three Weeks* by Elinor Glyn included a scene in which an English traveller is seduced by a Balkan queen on a tiger-skin rug. The *Daily Telegraph* condemned the book as squalid and the headmaster of Eton forbade his boys to read it, but it sold nine million copies that year.

Would you like to sin
With Elinor Glyn
On a tiger skin?
Or would you prefer
To err with her
On some other fur?
Popular rhyme of 1907

Mass production begins

IN HIS DETROIT FACTORY Henry Ford set up the world's first conveyor belt. Instead of a team of craftsmen building a car from start to finish, the job was broken down into the largest possible number of simple operations, each one of which was performed by a different worker. This system made production much quicker and cheaper and became the basis of most modern factory work, although it can be extremely boring for the workers involved. Ford promised that within a few years his conveyor belt would be turning out a car cheap enough for masses to afford.

I will build a motor car for the great multitude. It will be large enough for the family but small enough for the individual to run and care for. It will be constructed from the best materials, by the best men to be hired, after the simplest designs that modern engineering can devise. But it will be so low in price that no man making a good salary will be unable to own one – and enjoy with his family the blessing of hours of pleasure in God's great open spaces.
Henry Ford

Liners break all records

TWO OF THE WORLD'S largest and most luxurious ocean-going liners, the *Mauretania* and the *Lusitania*, were launched by the British firm of Cunard. On her maiden voyage to New York the *Lusitania* took the Blue Riband for the fastest Atlantic crossing away from the German liner, *Deutschland*, which had held it since 1900. Two years later the *Mauretania* was to cut the time for the voyage to four and a half days, a record that was to stand for the next 20 years.

Early twentieth-century high-speed travel: the Mauretania.

Some 'firsts' of 1907

A light-weight, portable domestic vacuum cleaner was designed by an American, Murray Spangler. It was made out of a tin can, a broomstick and a flour sack, connected to an electric motor. He sold the idea to a leather manufacturer W. Hoover, who put it on the market at a price of $75.

A helicopter, designed by a French bicycle dealer, managed to rise vertically into the air to a height of six feet (1.8m) and stay there for twenty seconds. It broke up on landing, but the twin-rotor design became the basis of the modern helicopter.

The first radio station to send out regular broadcasts was established on New York's 4th Avenue. The first programmes consisted entirely of gramophone music.

A calorimeter, which measured the energy value of foods in units called calories. Calorie-counting is now an indispensable part of many modern reducing diets.

Medical news

A TEAM of scientists at John Hopkins University in the USA managed to keep cells from animal tissues alive in a labora-tory. The technique of tissue culture was to become the basis of much modern investigation into the causes and cure for disease.

1908
Crisis in

The 'Young Turks' Rebel

DURING THE NINETEENTH CENTURY politicians in Europe had done much to reduce the extent of the Ottoman Empire, meddling in her internal affairs and encouraging those countries on the fringes of the Empire to break away. Resentment was high, especially among young, educated Turks, who blamed both foreign powers and their own government for the humiliations their country had suffered.

In July, junior officers in the Turkish army rose in rebellion against the corrupt and unpopular Sultan Abdul Hamid II, whose secretive nature had earned him the nickname 'Old Spider'. They dreamt of replacing the existing Muslim autocracy with a Western-style parliamentary government that would enable Turkey to compete on equal terms with the other great powers. It was the first of the modern nationalist revolutions. Terrified, Abdul Hamid gave in to the rebels and agreed to their demands. In the streets of Constantinople public rejoicing went on for days.

Europe reacts

UNFORTUNATELY FOR THE TURKS, their affairs were of interest to people other than themselves. For years Austria-Hungary had longed to annex out-right the two small provinces of Bosnia and Herzegovina that lay on the western borders of the Ottoman Empire and which were one day to form part of Yugoslavia. It was not greed for more territory that motivated her, but fear for her own future. For if Bosnia and Herzegovina, whose people were Slavs, were ever to become independent or be absorbed into the neighbouring Slav kingdom of Serbia, it would trigger off dreams of liberation among Austria's own Slavic peoples and put the whole Empire in danger. Better by far, argued Emperor Franz Josef and his advisers, to annex the troublesome area outright than to run that risk. Now with Turkey in chaos, the time seemed ripe.

A conspiracy

THE MAIN STUMBLING BLOCK was Russia, who was unlikely to tolerate such an increase in Austrian power. But the Foreign Minister, Count Aerenthal, thought he saw a way around that difficulty. Much of what happened over the next couple of months was kept secret and only came to light after the event. On 16 September he invited the Russian Foreign Minister, Izvolsky, to a clandestine meeting in the country. There they struck a bargain. It had long been Russia's ambition to seize control of the Dardenelles and the Bosporus, the two narrow outlets from the almost-landlocked Black Sea into the Mediterranean, a move that had always been blocked by Britain and France. Now it was agreed that Austria would back Russia's claims to the Straits if Russia turned a blind eye to the annexation of Bosnia and Herzegovina. Both statesmen left the meeting feeling that they had been very cunning and clever.

Crisis!

THE FIRST THE WORLD knew of this bargain was on 4 October, when news began to leak out that Austria-Hungary was about to make a surprise announcement.

On Tuesday Austria-Hungary will announce the formal annexation of Bosnia and Herzegovina.
Count Khevenbuhler-Metsch, the Austro-Hungarian Ambassador in Paris, had an audience with the President of the Republic at the Elysée Palace on Saturday afternoon and presented an autographed letter from his sovereign to M. Fallières, in which the Emperor Franz Josef announced his intention of Austria-Hungary with regard to Bosnia and Herzegovina . . . a similar announcement . . . is on its way to King Edward and will doubtless reach His Majesty at Balmoral tomorrow or Tuesday.
. .
I assumed at first that Great Britain and France had already been informed. Nothing of the sort has happened. These negotiations have been conducted in perfect secrecy. . .
All this had been done without the knowledge or consent of the other powers.
The Times, 5 October

It did not only come as a surprise to Britain and France but also to the Russian minister Izvolsky, who claimed that Aerenthal had promised to wait until Russia was ready to take action over the Straits. He accused Austria of blatantly breaking the spirit of their agreement, but as nothing had been put on paper, nothing could be proved. The blow to Russian pride was very great.

the Balkans

The Balkans, 1908.

Enter Serbia

LITTLE SERBIA was also outraged. To her, the annexation trampled on the rights of fellow Slavs. There were calls for revenge, and by the end of the year war between Austria and Serbia seemed very likely.

Countrymen, I thank you for your patriotic feelings, which I share. I hope that a few days hence you and I will have the opportunity of dying for King and Fatherland. Let us hope and believe it.
Speech by the Serbian Crown Prince, reported in *The Times*, 11 October

Storm clouds over Europe

MORE THAN JUST A SMALL WAR in the Balkans was at stake. If Serbia's ally, Russia should back her up – and given her wounded pride there was every chance that she would do so – a major conflict in Eastern Europe was in the offing. And if Germany came to the rescue of her ally, Austria, then the war might spread right across the continent. The omens at the end of 1908 seemed gloomy indeed.

The closing days of the year 1908, of which the most striking event has been the bloodless revolution in Turkey, have been such as to make it difficult for the historian to escape the general atmosphere of gloom and even anxiety that pervades the public mind of Europe. . . The world had almost forgotten since 1878 the dangers to peace that might arise from the Balkans peninsula; but one of the results of the crisis between Austria-Hungary and Russia has been a European crisis of which it is impossible to predict the end.
The Times, 31 December

World News

The Kaiser blunders

RELATIONS BETWEEN BRITAIN AND GERMANY, already tense because of naval rivalry, were made worse by an interview the Kaiser gave to the *Daily Telegraph*. Apparently, Wilhelm's intention had been to indicate his goodwill towards the British people, but his patronizing tone only succeeded in giving offence. Even if he meant well, many thoughtful people, inside and outside Germany, saw in his erratic and aggressive remarks signs of a mental instability that was very dangerous in so powerful a ruler.

You English are mad, mad, mad as March hares. What has come over you that you are so completely given over to suspicions quite unworthy of a great nation? What more can I do than I have done?

I have declared with all the emphasis at my command . . . that my heart is set upon peace, and that it is one of my dearest wishes to live on the best terms with England . . . but your press, or at any rate a considerable portion of it, bids the people of England to refuse my proffered hand, insinuates that the other holds a dagger. How can I convince a nation against its will?
Daily Telegraph, 28 October

Kaiser Wilhelm II of Germany in his favourite pose. The army had pride of place in Germany.

Belgium takes over the Congo

FIVE YEARS AFTER THE *BLACK DIARIES* revealed the scandalous conditions in Leopold's Congo, the Belgian Parliament confiscated it from the King and made it the property of the state. Belgium became Europe's seventh colonial power.

America elects a new President

TEDDY ROOSEVELT did not run for re-election but backed his Secretary for War, William H. Taft, as the next Republican candidate. Such was the outgoing President's prestige that Taft won easily in November against his Democrat rival, William Jennings Bryan. In his last major speech, Roosevelt begged Americans to realize that they were now a great power and should be willing to take their proper place at the centre of world affairs.

Empress of China dies

EMPRESS TZU-HSI OF CHINA died at the age of 73. For years she had dominated Chinese life and resisted all calls for reform and modernization. She was succeeded by her three-year-old nephew, P'u Yi. With nationalist feeling on the upsurge, however, it seemed unlikely that the Manchu dynasty could survive a long minority. Many thought that great change was coming to China.

Earthquake hits Calabria

A DEVASTATING EARTHQUAKE hit Southern Italy and Sicily in the last days of 1908. The towns of Reggio and Messina were reduced to rubble and swamped by gigantic tidal waves. Everywhere great fissures appeared in the ground. The death-toll was estimated at over 75,000.

A refugee from Reggio said that the shock was of incredible violence. Panic-stricken people, most of them in flimsy nightware, fled in all directions. He saw houses and churches toppling over into the streets, while the sea poured in.
Daily Telegraph, 31 December

Growing anger against the Lords

IN LONDON, the House of Lords continued to obstruct the Liberals whenever they could. Tempers ran high when a licensing law, which would have curbed the sale of alcoholic drinks and was dear to the temperance wing of the Liberal Party, was thrown out. The danger of a show-down between the two Houses of Parliament moved ever closer.

Unemployment on the rise

THE UNEMPLOYMENT RATE, which had been on the rise since Britain's economic supremacy ended around the turn of the century, reached 8 per cent, having risen from 2.5 per cent in 1900. At the same time prices were rising, while wages remained more or less static. What had cost £1 in 1900, now cost 24/–. Many working people were experiencing a real fall in their standard of living.

A rising political star: Lloyd George as seen by Vanity Fair.

A new Prime Minister

IN FEBRUARY CAMPBELL-BANNERMAN fell seriously ill and in April he resigned. He died soon afterwards. His place was taken by Herbert Henry Asquith, a cultured man who had been won over to the programme of very mild social reform. As Chancellor of the Exchequer, he had been responsible for bringing in old age pensions which were finally introduced early in 1909. The new Chancellor was the fiery radical, David Lloyd George, who was replaced at the Board of Trade by Winston Churchill.

200,000 demonstrate for votes for women

ONE OF THE LARGEST DEMONSTRATIONS ever held in London took place in Hyde Park in June. It was organized by the Suffragettes and police reckoned that over 200,000 people turned up, a fair number of them men. Although some of the men were sympathetic, others had come to jeer and heckle. There were scuffles and arrests. The meeting ended with a call to the government to bring in votes for women immediately.

A new kind of music

IN HIS COMPOSITION *The Book of the Hanging Gardens* the Austrian, Arnold Schoenberg, broke with centuries of European musical tradition, in which a piece of music was set in a particular key in order to produce a 'harmonious' melody. Schoenberg's 'atonal' music was based on a scale of 12 notes chosen by the composer, without a key centre. The work was met with violent hostility when first performed and people thought it sounded shockingly discordant at the time.

Sculpture causes a shock

AN EQUAL FURORE was caused by the American-born sculptor, Jacob Epstein, who had been commissioned to create a sculpture for the new headquarters of the British Medical Association in the Strand. His 18 figures representing the phases of human life were not at all in the dignified and realistically-detailed Victorian tradition that could be seen all over London. They were carved in a simpler, more austere style, which owed something to the influence of African art, and included representations of pregnant and breast-feeding women, which shocked many. Epstein went on to become one of the founding fathers of modern sculpture.

Two new children's books

TWO CHILDREN'S BOOKS were published this year which have since become enduring favourites. They were *The Wind in the Willows*, by Kenneth Grahame, which included a caustic comment on the motoring craze, and *Anne of Green Gables*, by Lucy M. Montgomery, which is set in Canada. It became the first of a whole series.

Call to revolution

A FRENCH PHILOSOPHER, Georges Sorel, published *Reflections on Violence*, in which he urged the trade unions to seize power by declaring a general strike and crippling the government. Only then could dreams of a more just and egalitarian society be realized. This doctrine became known as syndicalism and spread among trade unions in many countries especially France and Spain in the years before 1914.

Olympic Games held in London

THE 1908 OLYMPICS were held in London's White City stadium and were the first to be properly organized. Although the government had refused a subsidy, £60,000 had been raised by public subscription and over 300,000 spectators attended. British and American athletes were by far the most successful, winning first place in 82 events between them. A number of athletics records were made that were to stand into the 1920s. Contests in soccer and rowing were introduced for the first time. One popular event that has since disappeared from the Olympics was the tug of war, which was won by the Liverpool Police.

First black boxing champion

WHEN JACK JOHNSON of the USA beat Canadian Tommy Burns in Sydney, Australia, on Boxing Day, he became the first black boxing champion ever. He held the title until he lost to Jess Willard of Kansas in 1915. His success was unpopular among many white Americans, especially in the Deep South, and there were even demonstrations in some cities when the result of the Sydney match was announced.

The champion Jack Johnson in 1908.

Some important developments for the future

TWO FRENCH SCIENTISTS, Calmetter and Guerin, isolated the bovine TB bacillus in a cow, which would one day make possible the routine testing of cattle and the provision of pure, tuberculin-tested milk.

Ammonia was first produced from nitrogen, which was to become the basis of modern, synthetic fertilizers. Although these have increased crop yields, many people now believe they have been a mixed blessing and may cause damage to the environment and to the people who eat the food grown in them.

In Britain, Sir Archibald Garrod discovered that a rare disorder, alkaptonuria, was due to an inborn, inherited metabolic defect. This triggered off research that was eventually to lead to the discovery that other diseases like haemophilia and some types of muscular dystrophy were inherited, and opened the way to genetic counselling.

Some 'firsts' of 1908

Geiger counter for measuring levels of radioactivity.

Electric light bulb with a tungsten filament, which would burn much brighter and last much longer than earlier ones, which had burned osmium or carbon. Most modern light bulbs still use tungsten.

Barium meal X-rays Normal X-rays only give a picture of hard tissues like bone and pass straight through soft tissues like those of the intestine. It was discovered that if a patient swallowed barium sulphate, it then became possible to take X-ray photographs of the stomach and intestine. This was particularly useful for detecting gastric ulcers and was in regular use until it was replaced by the ultrasonic scan in the 1970s.

Pioneer of flight: Wilbur Wright at the controls of his flying machine during the Wright brothers' European tour.

American becomes world's first air crash victim

ON 17 SEPTEMBER Lieutenant Thomas E. Selfridge became the first man ever to die in an air crash, when the biplane in which he was a passenger lost a propellor blade and plunged to the ground from a height of 75 feet. The plane, built by the Wright brothers and piloted by Orville Wright, was on a demonstration flight at an army base in Virginia, where senior army officers were debating whether the new flying machines had any military use and would be worth investing in. Orville Wright himself was badly injured but expected to recover.

The crash did nothing to dampen the growing enthusiasm for flying in both Europe and the USA. In October Wilbur Wright visited Europe to show off his latest model, which was far more advanced than the 1903 one. At Le Mans in France he stayed up in the air for over an hour and the last doubts among Europeans about the future of flight were swept away. A frantic race began to catch up with the Americans.

Rising discontent in Europe

BENEATH THE GLITTERING SURFACE of Europe, where the lifestyles of the rich and well-born made the headlines, serious cracks were appearing in the fabric of society. Poverty was still widespread and living standards were tending to fall as competition between the industrial nations hotted up. As literacy rose, the poor and downtrodden were less inclined to suffer in silence. In 1909 several European countries experienced the opening shots of what might prove to be the coming class war.

The scourge of the rich: a Punch *cartoon on the People's Budget.*

The people's budget

IN BRITAIN Chancellor Lloyd George needed to raise £15 million to pay for old age pensions and new battleships. His annual budget introduced in April raised taxes all round, but the biggest shock was caused by a new levy on the value of land, payable every time it changed hands. The yield would be small – less, probably, than the cost of collecting the tax – but the principle was revolutionary. Land values were rising so fast that the great hereditary landowners, most of whom were already fabulously wealthy, grew richer by the year without even lifting a finger. They saw it as their right, but Lloyd George saw them as parasites. It was time, he argued, that they contributed to the common good.

This is a War Budget. It is for raising money to wage implacable war against poverty and squalidness. I cannot help believing that before this generation has passed away, we shall have advanced a great step towards that good time when poverty, wretchedness and the human degradation that has always followed in its camp will be as remote to the people of this country as the wolves that once infested its forests.
Lloyd George to the Commons

No country, however rich, can permanently afford to have quartered upon its revenue a class which declines to do the duty it was called on to perform.
Lloyd George at Limehouse, Liverpool, 30 July

The Lords rebel

THE LORDS WERE HORRIFIED. When the budget came up from the Commons, they threw it out. The Liberals threw the issue open to the people and called a general election for January 1910. The crisis that had been brewing since 1906 had arrived. To the peers, the budget was the first round in an attack on property rights that would lead to socialism and the end of society as they knew it. To Lloyd George and his supporters, it was the start of a battle for a fairer society.

Let them realise what they are doing. They are forcing a revolution, and they will get it. The Lords may decree a revolution, but the people will direct it. If they begin, issues will be raised that they little dream of. . . The question will be asked whether five hundred men, ordinary men chosen accidentally from among the unemployed, should override the judgement . . . of millions of people who are engaged in the industry that makes the wealth of this country.
Lloyd George in Newcastle, 10 October

Crisis in Spain

THE CLASS CONFLICT in Britain was still a war of words. In Spain, where poverty was even more widespread, events took a more violent turn. The centre of discontent was Barcelona, Spain's largest industrial city and the capital of the province of Catalonia, that had its own distinctive culture and language. Here the twin pressures of poverty and regional pride mingled to form a volatile mixture, for Catalonians of all classes hated control from Madrid.

War

Barcelona's tragic week

A CRISIS CAME IN JULY, when reservists were called up to fight in Spanish Morocco. On 26 July the local syndicalist unions called a general strike against mobilization and Barcelona ground to a halt. Trams and trains stopped running and for nearly a week the city was cut off from the rest of Spain. Troops from the local garrison refused to fire on strikers and joined them instead. A wave of popular hatred against the Roman Catholic Church, which was seen as the symbol of Spain's backwardness, rose to the surface. Over 50 convents and churches were burnt down and the monks and nuns turned out. Graves were dug up in an attempt to prove that their occupants had been tortured to death by fanatical priests.

A street in Barcelona at the end of July. In spite of the rumours, the damage to property was much greater than the loss of life.

Into the future

ALTHOUGH MOST OF THE STRIKES and revolutions of 1909 collapsed in the end, life at the end of the opening decade of the twentieth century seemed far less secure for the privileged classes of Europe than it had seemed at the beginning. It was just as clear that they would not give up their privileges without a fight. Everywhere the future of Europe suddenly seemed very uncertain.

Myth or reality?

THE VIOLENCE sent waves of horror through Spain's wealthier classes and fear bred exaggeration. While Barcelona remained cut off, dreadful rumours circulated about what was happening there during what became known as the 'Semana Tragica' (Tragic Week). However there were no massacres, for hatred of the Church was directed against property rather than people. Of the deaths, only three were priests. Almost all the others were strikers themselves. In the end, troops from other parts of Spain were sent in and the revolution in Barcelona was

crushed. So frightened had the ruling classes been that they took their revenge by executing a well-known revolutionary thinker, Francisco Ferrer, who had played no part in events in Barcelona. He had been in England at the time on a lecture tour!

Blind-drunk with blood, wine, dynamite and petroleum and with the desire to kill for killing's sake, the rebels destroyed convents and killed the inmates. Who can tell the number of dead, wounded or burnt who lie beneath the ruins?. . . Spare me the recital of details of the martyrdom of the monks and the ill-treatment of the nuns. . . I will only say that many died at the foot of the altar stabbed by hundreds of evil women.

From a conservative Spanish newspaper, published after the end of the Barcelona uprising.

Strikes spread

A WAVE OF STRIKES that had begun in France in 1906 reached a climax too, when civil servants, post office workers and primary school teachers came out in the summer and called on other workers to declare a general strike in their support. Prime Minister Clemneceau brought in the army and the strikes were brutally crushed, but not before the government itself had been forced to resign. In Sweden over 500,000 workers came out on strike. Although the total population was only 5.5 million, society did not collapse, because upper-class volunteers organized brigades to keep essential services going. After a month, the strike broke when the government threatened to deprive strikers of their pension rights.

World News

Threat of war over the Balkans

TENSION ROSE in the Balkans in the early months of 1909. In January, Serbia called up reservists, and threatening speeches against Austria-Hungary were made in the Belgrade Parliament. Germany egged her ally on to stand up to Serbia, who in turn looked to Russia for support. Alarmed, the British Foreign Secretary, Sir Edward Grey, tried to mediate. After three months of mounting threats of war, Russia and Serbia stepped down and Austria kept the two disputed provinces. The immediate crisis had passed but the bitterness remained. Russia had gained nothing except the determination never to be treated like that again. At a congress of Slavic peoples held in St Petersburg that summer, she told the Balkan representatives to wait patiently while she rebuilt her army. The time was coming when she would help them fight to free themselves from Austrian or Turkish rule. Relations between Russia and Germany, once friendly, had deteriorated.

Row over the North Pole

IN APRIL an American, Commander Robert Peary, sent out a message that he had become the first man ever to reach the North Pole and was now on his way home. His claim was contested by another American, Dr Frederick Cooke, who now swore that he had reached the Pole a year earlier. When Peary got back, a full-scale public row erupted between the two men, both of whom accused the other of being a liar. In the end, both an independent Danish committee of inquiry and the US Congress found in favour of Peary, who is remembered today as the first man to reach the North Pole.

Sultan deposed

THE YOUNG TURKS tightened their grip on the country. When Sultan Abdul Hamid tried to hit back in April, he was deposed in favour of his brother, Mahmud V. The dismantling of Islamic customs began. Women, for instance, were discouraged from wearing the veil. The dream of liberation for the non-Turkish peoples of the Empire was soon shattered, however, as the Young Turks proved to be as chauvinistic as any Sultan had been. They were, wrote the British ambassador in Constantinople, intent on 'pounding non-Turkish elements in a Turkish mortar'. Hopes of democracy also faded, as the Young Turk government, which had started by holding elections, steadily became more and more autocratic.

Unemployment Exchanges set up

IN BRITAIN, a report by a young civil servant, William Beveridge, made quite an impact in government circles. In 'Unemployment, a Problem of Industry' he argued that some of the worst poverty in Britain was to be found among those like dockers and building workers who were usually hired on a casual basis and could be laid off for weeks at a time when trade was bad. Beveridge suggested that Labour Exchanges were the answer, where the unemployed could find out easily what casual work was available, and where the needs of employers and workers could be matched up. This idea was taken up by Winston Churchill in 1909 and the first Labour Exchanges opened in February 1910.

South Africa gains dominion status

IN SEPTEMBER an act was passed uniting the four South African states into the Union of South Africa and giving the new country dominion status. Citizens of both Boer and English descent were to have equal rights, but there was no guarantee of equal treatment for the black or coloured races. The Boers had indeed won the peace.

We want eight

GERMANY had now caught up with Britain in the building of Dreadnoughts. In panic, the Admiralty asked for six more to be built at once. The press, now in the vanguard of anti-German feeling, stirred up public opinion with the slogan: 'We Want Eight and We Won't Wait'. The government gave in to the clamour and eight new super-battleships were commissioned at a cost of £9 million. To raise the money for them was one of the aims of the People's Budget.

We stand in a crisis of national peril, such as for two hundred years has never threatened us in peace or war. By an act of moral treachery, which would justify us in armed reprisals now, a foreign power has doubled its naval programme in secret and has gained six months start in a conspiracy against our life. . . We must fight before 1910 – while we have a full margin of power in our hand, or build eight Dreadnoughts now. There is no third way.
The Observer, 21 March

Left: *The first man to reach the North Pole – official! Peary and his dogs.*

Right: *A suffragette poster.*

Suffragettes hit the headlines

THEIR FRUSTRATION MOUNTING, Suffragettes turned to more dramatic tactics. They heckled Liberal speakers. They broke the windows of 10 Downing Street and chained themselves to the railings of public buildings. One woman attacked Churchill with a dog-whip. Some observers argued that such behaviour only did the women's cause harm. Suffragettes were frequently arrested and imprisoned and in July a Miss Wallace-Dunlop who went on a hunger strike in her cell was released, so that the prison authorities would not have the embarrassment of her dying in custody. Soon more and more imprisoned Suffragettes were refusing to eat and forcible feeding was introduced. So brutal were the methods that public sympathy began to swing round to the Suffragettes.

Sport and the Arts

Russian stars come to Paris

A RUSSIAN LIVING IN PARIS, Serge Diaghilev, founded a company to bring Russian ballet to the rest of the world. In his first season he brought over two of Russia's most famous stars, Anna Pavlova and Vaslav Nijinsky. His productions were much more exuberant and colourful than the classical ballet Europe was used to and drew large and enthusiastic audiences. Later Diaghilev was to introduce daring new ballets like *The Firebird* and *The Rite of Spring* to music by the Russian composer Stravinsky.

New architecture in Berlin

ONE OF THE MOST FAMOUS EXAMPLES of the new architecture went up in Berlin in 1909. It was a factory designed for the AEG electrical company by the architect Peter Behrens. It was built of concrete, with a steel frame that was clearly visible from the outside and was meant to be part of the design. Because most of the weight was taken by the frame, glass panels were used instead of ordinary walls which made the interior light and airy, unlike most factories, which were dark and smelly inside.

New London store opened

WHEN AMERICAN BUSINESSMAN, Gordon Selfridge, came to England, he was shocked by how dark and poky most shops were. In 1909 he opened England's first proper department store in London's Oxford Street. It carried £100,000 worth of goods and employed 1800 staff. Selfridge intended to make shopping fun, and his store became part of the glittering image of the age, although, of course, only the wealthy could shop there.

In my store women can realise some of their dreams. Here they come as guests, not customers to be bullied into buying. This is not a shop, it is a social experience.
Gordon Selfridge

Girl Guides founded

SIR ROBERT (later Lord) Baden-Powell, the hero of Mafeking, had founded the Boy Scouts in 1907 to teach boys to be hardy and resourceful and of service to others. When they held a big rally at Crystal Palace in 1909, so many girls came with their brothers and asked to be allowed to join that Baden-Powell set up the Girl Guides for them. It was run at first by his sister, Agnes. From the start the girls did much the same strenuous things as the boys which some people found rather shocking, but the movement went on from strength to strength. The name was taken from a famous cavalry unit in the Indian army, the Corps of Guides.

Football match ends with violence

CROWDS AT EDWARDIAN sporting events were usually large but nearly always well-behaved. Sometimes, however, when passions ran high, there were outbreaks of hooliganism at football matches similar to those that plague the modern game.

The Preston North End team, which played a drawn game with Sheffield Wednesday at Owlerton on Saturday, were violently treated at the conclusion of the match by a crowd of spectators who were dissatisfied with the result.
Councillor Houghton, who was in charge of the Preston team gave an *Express* representative the following account of what took place:
Immediately we left in a charabanc we were pelted with showers of clinkers, cinders and stones from crowds of excited people who congregated in the streets.
Nearly every player was struck. Lyon was hit behind the head with a heavy stone, and sustained a heavy scalp wound. Among the missiles which struck the players were two large clinkers, raw potatoes, a lump of billiard chalk, a jagged piece of earthenware, a penny, and a pearly-handled penknife.
The outside passengers of every tramcar we passed deliberately leaned over and spat in our faces.
Daily Express, 29 January

Some cultural events of 1909
Portrait of Adolf Loos, by the young Czech artist, Oskar Kokoschka. This was the first of his 'psychological portraits', designed to show the inner character rather than the outward appearance of the sitter.

Ann Veronica, a novel by H.G. Wells about the new 'independent' woman.

The Robie House in Chicago, designed for a wealthy client by Frank Lloyd Wright. It was the first complete example of an open-plan house, designed to be functional rather than decorative.

Strife, by John Galsworthy, a play about an industrial dispute in a tin plate factory.

The first Fords take to the road

THE FIRST OF FORD'S new, cheap motor cars – the Model T – rolled off the production line. They were nicknamed 'Tin Lizzies' and cost $950. Compared with other cars of the time, they were cheap but still beyond the pockets of most ordinary people. Ford insisted, however, that as his conveyor belts became more efficient, the price would keep on going down, which is indeed what happened.

The 'people's car': one of the first Tin Lizzies.

No longer an island

THERE WAS MUCH SPECULATION in the press about what Man's conquest of the air would mean for the future, especially for an island like Britain. Not only would civilian travel be revolutionized in the long run, but the sea would no longer be the protection against invasion it had always been in the past.

The first plane across the channel. Bleriot landing on the cliff-tops of Dover.

Frenchman flies the Channel

INSPIRED BY THE WRIGHT BROTHERS' visit the year before, French aircraft research was racing ahead. The *Daily Mail* offered a £1000 prize to the first man to fly across the Channel. On 25 July, in a monoplane made of poplar and ash wood tied together by piano strings and weighing only 45 lb. (20.4 kg), a Frenchman, Louis Bleriot, succeeded, to be greeted at Dover by an excited crowd. The journey had taken just 37 minutes. As he had no compass on board, he had had to find his direction by following the ships below. In spite of the progress made since 1903, flying was still a very risky business.

Ten minutes have gone. I have passed the destroyer, and I turn my head to see if I am going in the right direction. I am amazed. There is nothing to be seen, neither the destroyer, nor France, nor England. I am alone. I can see nothing at all – rien du tout! For ten minutes I am lost. It is strange to be here alone, unguided . . . in the air over the middle of the Channel. I touch nothing. My hands and feet rest lightly on the levers. I let the aeroplane take its own course. I care not whither it goes. . . And then, twenty minutes after I have left the French coast, I see the green cliffs of Dover and the castle.
Bleriot's account of the flight, published in the *Daily Mail*, 26 July

Medical breakthrough

THE FIRST EFFECTIVE TREATMENT for the venereal disease, syphilis, which had killed and disfigured hundreds of thousands over the centuries, was discovered by a German bacteriologist, Paul Ehrlich. This was salvarsan, a compound containing arsenic. Many hailed it as a miracle drug, but others condemned it as an encouragement to sin.

Some 'firsts' of 1909

Cars with shock-absorbers. Before this, cars had springs copied from those in horse-drawn carriages, which made motoring very uncomfortable.

A kind of plastic was invented in Belgium by Leo Baekeland. Called bakelite, it was very brittle and breakable compared with modern plastics. It was used for gramophone records, telephones and electrical insulation.

Light-weight but tough aluminium alloys were manufactured in Germany. They were to become the materials out of which modern aircraft were made.

Time Chart

World News	Sport and the Arts	Science and Technology
1900 (January) Battle of Spion Kop. (February) Relief of Kimberley and Ladysmith. Labour Representation Committee formed. (May) Relief of Mafeking. (June) Boxers besiege foreign legations in Beijing. US annexes Hawaiian Islands. (July) Assassination of King Umberto of Italy. Second German Naval Law is passed. (August) Boxers defeated. (October) Khaki election in Britain.	Second modern Olympic Games open. *Daily Express* begins production.	(April) Paris Exhibition opens. First electrified underground line opens in London. Trial flight of the *Graf Zepplin*.
1901 (January) Twentieth century officially opens. Death of Queen Victoria and accession of Edward VII. Commonwealth of Australia comes into being. Building of 'blockhouses' begins in South Africa. (July) Taff Vale judgement. (September) Assassination of President McKinley of USA; Theodore Roosevelt becomes President. Publication of Rowntree's study on poverty in York. Anglo-German alliance negotiations broken off.	(April) Record crowd attends FA Cup Final at Crystal Palace. Frank Lloyd Wright publishes *The Art and Craft of the Machine*.	Marconi transmits radio signal from Cornwall to Newfoundland.
1902 (January) Anglo-Japanese treaty. (April) Russian Minister of Interior is assassinated. Treaty of Vereeniging ends Boer War. (July) Balfour becomes Prime Minister. Australian women get the vote. (August) French general election; Combes becomes Prime Minister. Coronation of Edward VII. (December) Education Act in Britain.	Moscow Art Theatre performs Gorky's *The Lower Depths*. Caruso makes first gramophone recording. Sir Arthur Conan Doyle's *The Hound of the Baskervilles* published.	Pierre and Marie Curie isolate radium. (December) Aswam Dam opens.
1903 (March) Religious orders dissolved in France. (May) Edward VII's visit to Paris. Chamberlain's tariff reform speech in Birmingham. Casement reveals evidence of Congo atrocities. (July) President Loubet's state visit to Britain. (September) Lib-Lab Pact signed. Women's Social and Political Union founded. (November) US-Panama treaty signed. Russian Social Democratic congress in London leads to split in party.	(October) First baseball World Series. (November) First MCC-sponsored tour begins. *The Great Train Robbery* made in the US.	(August) Speed limit of 20 mph introduced in Britain, and registration of motorcars made compulsory. (December) Orville Wright makes first flight.
1904 (January) US intervention in Dominican Republic. Herero rising in South-West Africa begins. (February) Russo-Japanese War begins. (April) Entente Cordiale signed. (May) Japanese defeat Russians on Yalu River. Chinese indentured labourers in South Africa. (June) Siege of Port Arthur begins. (August) Younghusband expedition reaches Lhasa. (October) Dogger Bank incident. Commissioning of HMS *Dreadnought*. (November) Roosevelt re-elected. (December) Pacific Fleet sunk at Port Arthur.	*Daily Mirror* launched. (May) Third Olympic Games opens at St Louis. *Peter Pan*, by J.M. Barrie, first produced.	New York Subway opens. Pavlov receives Nobel Prize.

Time Chart

World News	Sport and the Arts	Science and Technology
1905		
(January) Bloody Sunday in St Petersburg. Fall of Port Arthur. (March) Battle of Mukden. Kaiser's Tangier speech. (May) Battle of Tsushima. (June) Resignation of Delcassé. (September) Treaty of Portsmouth. (October) *Potemkin* mutiny. General strike in Russia; Petrograd Soviet set up. October Manifesto. First Suffragettes go to gaol. (November) Norway becomes independent. (December) Unrest in India.	(September) 'Les Fauves' exhibition in Paris. World's first cinema opens in Pittsburgh. Jack Hobbs plays first season for Surrey.	Einstein publishes *The Special Theory of Relativity*.
1906		
(January) Algeciras Conference opens. Liberals win landslide election victory. (April) San Francisco earthquake. (May) First Duma meets in Russia. (July) Dreyfus rehabilitated. First Duma dissolved by the Tsar. HMS *Dreadnought* launched.	Upton Sinclair's *The Jungle* published in the US. (June) First Grand Prix held at Le Mans.	(March) Electrification of the London Underground completed. (May) Simplon Tunnel opens. (December) First radio broadcast in America.
1907		
(January) Universal male suffrage in Austria-Hungary. Territorial Army Act in Britain. (April) Second Duma meets. (June) Second Duma dissolved. Female suffrage in Norway. (August) Anglo-Russian Convention. Stuttgart Socialist congress.	*Playboy of the Western World* by J.M. Synge causes riot when performed in Dublin. Cubist exhibition in Paris.	Ford begins mass-production in Detroit. *Lusitania* wins Blue Riband for fastest Atlantic crossing.
1908		
(April) Resignation of Campbell-Bannerman. H.H. Asquith becomes Prime Minister. (July) Young Turks revolt. (August) Old Age Pensions Act in Britain. Belgium takes over the Congo. (September) Secret meeting between Aerenthal and Izvolsky. (October) Austrian annexation of Bosnia and Herzegovina. Kaiser's *Daily Telegraph* interview. (November) Taft elected President of USA.	Schoenberg's first atonal compositions performed. (June) Epstein's figures unveiled. (July) Olympic Games held in London. (December) Jack Johnson becomes World Heavyweight champion.	Wright brothers visit Europe. First light bulbs with tungsten filament introduced.
1909		
Threat of Austro-Serbian war. (March) Serbia steps down and Balkan crisis ends. 'We Want Eight' crisis in Britain. (April) Peoples' Budget introduced. Abdication of Sultan Abdul Hamid II. Peary reaches North Pole. (July) Rising in Barcelona. Fall of French Government. (September) Union of South Africa Act. Labour Exchange Act. (November) Lords reject budget; Parliament dissolved.	Diaghilev brings Pavlova and Nijinsky to Paris. Behren's AEG factory opens.	Bleriot flies the Channel.

Key figures of the decade

Abdul Hamid II (1842-1915)

Sultan of Turkey 1876-1909, he opposed all movements for liberalization or local autonomy within his Empire. Deposed by the Young Turks in 1909 and exiled from the capital for ever.

Herbert Henry Asquith (1855-1928)

Barrister, who became a Liberal MP in 1886. A 'Liberal Imperialist' during the Boer War, he made his peace with the anti-war wing of the party, was appointed Chancellor of the Exchequer in 1905 and took the first measures towards the foundation of the welfare state. An opponent of women's suffrage. Prime Minister 1908-15.

Arthur James Balfour (1848-1930)

Member of politically-influential Cecil family and nephew of Lord Salisbury. made his reputation in the tricky job of Chief Secretary for Ireland 1886-92. Prime Minister 1902-5, suffered crushing defeat in 1906 election. Leader of the Conservative opposition during the battle to restrict the powers of the House of Lords 1909-11.

Sir Roger Casement (1864-1916)

Irishman, who served in British consular service 1892-1911 and who came to public notice when he uncovered the scandalous treatment of Africans in the rubber trade in King Leopold's Congo in 1903. Became a convert to Irish nationalism and in 1914 sought German aid for an uprising against British rule there. Returned to Ireland on a German submarine in April 1916 to take part in the Easter Rising, was arrested and hanged for treason.

Joseph Chamberlain (1836-1914)

Self-made Birmingham businessman, entered Parliament as a Liberal in 1876 and was often tipped as Gladstone's successor as leader. Split with the Party in 1886 over Irish Home Rule Bill and led the Liberal-Unionist faction in the Commons, which was eventually absorbed into the Conservative party. As Colonial Secretary 1895-1903, he was closely involved in the Boer War 1899-1902. Favoured an alliance with Germany as the alternative to Splendid Isolation. Took up cause of Imperial Preference and tariff reform in 1903, which helped to lose the Conservatives the 1906 election.

Sir Henry Campbell-Bannerman (1836-1908)

Wealthy Scottish businessman, who became Liberal leader in the Commons in 1898. An opponent of the Boer War. Prime Minister 1905-8, he resigned on the grounds of ill health. His strength as a Prime Minister was his ability to hold together a team of strong-minded personalities. A supporter of moderate social reform.

Marie Curie (1867-1934)

Polish-born scientist, who studied in Paris and married Pierre Curie, a French professor of physics, in 1895. The Curies did important research into the nature of radioactivity and discovered two new radioactive elements, radium and polonium. In 1902 the Curies were awarded the Nobel Prize for physics jointly with A.H. Becquerel.

Edward VII (1841-1910)

Eldest son of Queen Victoria and Prince Albert. King of Britain and Emperor of India 1901-10. Died in the middle of the constitutional crisis over proposals to reform the House of Lords, that arose as a result of the People's Budget 1909.

Albert Einstein (1879-1955)

German mathematician, whose Theory of Relativity, first published in 1905 and elaborated in 1915, laid the groundwork for the development of nuclear science and the atom bomb. As a Jew he fled from Germany in 1933, when Hitler came to power, and spent the rest of his life in the USA.

Admiral John Fisher (1841-1920)

Career naval officer, who joined at 13 and rose through the ranks. Always interested in new techniques and suspicious of German intentions after the Naval Laws of 1897 and 1900, he updated the British navy and commissioned the first Dreadnoughts.

Henry Ford (1863-1947)

Self-made American industrialist and founder of the Ford Motor Company of Detroit. His introduction of the idea of the cheap mass-produced cars ushered in the age of the modern industry and assembly-line production. Conditions of employment in his early factories were far in advance of most others of his day, but he remained a life-long opponent of trade unions. He brought in the eight-hour day and an employee profit-sharing scheme in 1914.

Franz Josef I (1830-1916)

Emperor of Austria 1848-1916. Self-styled monarch of the 'old school' who opposed any changes that would hasten the break-up of his ramshackle multi-national empire or weaken the Emperor's authority. Apart

Key figures of the decade

from this, his rule was generally tolerant and he remained surprisingly popular until his death, only 18 months before the final collapse of the Austro-Hungarian Empire.

Rudyard Kipling (1865-1936)

Born in India, which supplied the inspiration for his first successful writing *Plain Tales from the Hills* (1888) and *The Jungle Book* (1894). Became the poet of the duties and hardships of Imperialism, including 'Barrack Room Ballards' (1892) and 'The White Man's Burden' (1899), although he was never the simple, unthinking jingoist that later generations often painted him and was often critical of British arrogance or complacency.

Horatio H. Kitchener (1850-1916)

Career Army officer who rose to prominence in the 1890s. Chief of Staff to Lord Roberts in South Africa December 1899 – November 1900 and then Commander-in-Chief there. Responsible for the much criticized system of blockhouses and concentration camps, which gradually wore down Boer resistance.

Leopold II (1835-1909)

King of the Belgians 1865-1909 and personal ruler of the Congo 1885-1908.

David Lloyd George (1863-1945)

Welsh solicitor of humble origins, who was elected Liberal MP for Carnarvon in 1890. A fiery orator, a pro-Boer 1899-1902 and chief spokesman of the radical, reforming wing of the Liberal Party. President of the Board of Trade 1905-8, Chancellor of the Exchequer 1908-15. He was Prime Minister from 1916-1922.

Guglielmo Marconi (1874-1937)

Italian inventor, who sent the first wireless signal over a mile in 1895 and across the Atlantic in 1901. Up until his death he continued to play a leading part in the development of commercial radio and wireless telegraph services.

Nicholas II (1868-1918)

Last Tsar of Russia 1894-1917. Fanatical believer in Russian autocratic tradition, who was nevertheless an indecisive ruler and a poor judge of men. His failure to see the need for change brought Russia to the brink of revolution in 1905 and led to the granting of a parliamentary constitution in the October Manifesto. Murdered with his family by the Bolsheviks in 1918.

Emmeline Pankhurst (1858-1928)

Widow of a barrister and founder of the Suffragette movement, Women's Social and Political Union, which resorted to increasingly militant tactics between 1905 and 1914. Spent time in prison in 1908, 1909, 1911-12 (for breaking windows) and 1913-14 (for arson). Went on hunger strike in 1912. During the 1914-18 war she encouraged women to prove their worthiness for the vote by volunteering for service in industry and the armed forces.

Theodore Roosevelt (1858-1919)

American Republican politician. Under-secretary for the Navy 1897-8 he did much to build up the US navy and make it ready for the war with Spain, which he welcomed with enthusiasm and took part in personally. Reforming, anti-corruption Governor of New York State 1899-1900 and Vice-President 1900-1, becoming President on McKinley's sudden death. As President, he continued the twin policies of reform at home and belligerence abroad, including

the seizure of the Panama Canal zone from Colombia in 1903. Awarded Nobel Peace Prize 1906 for his role in bringing Russian-Japanese war to an end.

George Bernard Shaw (1856-1950)

Irish-born dramatist and member of the moderate socialist Fabian Society, who used his plays as a vehicle for his ideas. Among his most famous works, which are often performed today, are *Arms and the Man* (1894), *Major Barbara* (1905), *The Doctor's Dilemma* (1906), *Pygmalion* (1913), and *St Joan* (1923). Won the Nobel Prize for Literature in 1925.

Admiral Alfred von Tirpitz (1849-1930)

Career naval officer and favourite of the Kaiser, who served as German Naval Minister 1897-1916. Believing that only possession of a strong navy would enable Germany to compete against Britain, he piloted the 1897 and 1900 Naval Bills through the Reichstag and after 1906 insisted that Germany build a fleet of Dreadnoughts.

Leon Trotsky (1879-1940)

Real name Lev Bronstein. Russian Marxist revolutionary, who spent the years 1900-5 in exile and returned to join in the 1905 uprising and head the Petrograd Soviet. Imprisoned and exiled again in 1906, he came back again in 1917 and played a key role in the new Communist state until he was exiled once again by his rival, Stalin, in 1929. He was murdered in Mexico by a Stalinist agent in 1940.

Wilhelm II (1859-1941)

Emperor of Germany 1888-1918. Son of Emperor Frederick III and Princess Vicky, eldest daughter of Queen Victoria. Proud of Germany's economic and military might

69

Key figures of the decade

and a lover of military display, his aggressive behaviour helped brand him as a war-monger among his contemporaries and increase tensions in Europe. Forced to abdicate in November 1918, he spent the rest of his life in exile in Holland.

Frank Lloyd Wright (1869-1959)

American architect and pioneer of the use of modern materials to create a new style advocating light and space that was to have such an influence on twentieth-century architecture.

Orville Wright (1871-1948) and Wilbur Wright (1867-1912)

Owners of a bicycle shop in Dayton, Ohio, who experimented first with gliders and then with motorized aeroplanes, before they succeeded in putting the first one into the air in 1903. It took several years for the Wrights' invention to be fully accepted at home and abroad, but after 1908 the age of modern aviation took off. Although the brothers took little part in further developments, Orville lived to see his early dreams result in planes that could fly at over 500 miles per hour.

Books for further reading

European and world history
P. Fleming, *The Siege at Peking*, Oxford, 1984
C. Petrie, *The Drift to World War I*, London, 1968
A.J.P. Taylor, *The Last of Old Europe*, London, 1976
B. Tuchman, *The Proud Tower*, New York, 1966
P. Vansittart, *Voices 1870-1914*, London, 1984
N. Westwood, *Russo-Japanese War*, London, 1973

British history
R. Cecil, *Life in Edwardian England*, London, 1972

K. Fenning, *Edwardian Britain: A Society in Transition*, Glasgow, 1980
J. McMillan, *The Way We Were 1900-1914*, London, 1978
D. Read, *Edwardian England*, London, 1972
R. West, *1900*, London, 1982

Biographies and autobiographies
There are hundreds of biographies dealing with leading figures of this period. A few of the most readable are:
M. Balfour, *The Kaiser and his Times*, London, 1964
H.K. Beale, *Theodore Roosevelt and the Rise of America to World Power*, New York, 1956

G. Brook-Shepherd, *Uncle of Europe: The Social and Diplomatic Life of Edward VII*, London, 1975
E. Curie, *Marie Curie*, London, 1962
J. Grigg, *Lloyd George, the People's Champion 1902-1911*, London, 1978
E. Jones, *The Life and Work of Sigmund Freud*, London, 1964
L.E. Jones, *An Edwardian Youth*, London, 1956
R. Massie, *Nicholas and Alexandra*, London, 1968
E. Pankhurst, *My Own Story*, London, 1979
D. Reitz, *Commando: A Boer Journal of the Boer War*, London, 1931

Acknowledgments

The Bettman Archive for page 38 (left); the Bridgeman Art Library for page 3; the Hulton Picture Company for the front and back covers, the frontispiece and pages 4, 13, 16, 25, 35, 42, 43, 46, 52, 53, 58 and 59; the Mansell Collection for pages 18, 20, 22, 26, 61 and 62; the Mary Evans Picture Library for the front cover (colour) and pages 5, 6, 7, 11, 12, 14, 15, 17, 21, 23, 25, 27, 29, 30, 33, 34, 36, 37, 38 (right), 41 (both), 45, 47, 50, 51, 56, 57, 60, 63 and 65 (both); Mary Evans/Sigmund Freud Copyrights for page 10; and the National Film Archive, London for page 28. The maps on pages 3, 19 and 55 were drawn by Robert F. Brien.

Index

Numbers in **bold** type refer to illustrations

Index